Make Ahead
PALEO

healthy gluten-, grain-, and dairy-free
recipes ready *when* and *where* you are

Tammy Credicott

National Best-Selling
Author of
Paleo Indulgences
&
The Healthy Gluten-Free Life

VICTORY BELT PUBLISHING INC.
Las Vegas

First Published in 2013 by Victory Belt Publishing Inc.

ISBN 13: 978-1-936608-37-9

This book is for educational purposes. The publisher and author of this cookbook are not responsible in any manner whatsoever for any adverse effects arising directly or indirectly as a result of the information provided in this book.

Printed in the USA

RRD 0113

Cover photographs: Tammy Credicott (food) and Justin Earl Photography (author photo)

Cover design: Kate Miller Design and Victory Belt Publishing Inc.

Interior photographs: Tammy Credicott

Food styling: Tammy Credicott

Interior design: Kate Miller Design and Victory Belt Publishing

"Go cook something...
anything!
Just get in the kitchen
and make some food."

–Tammy Credicott

"Tammy's fabulous grain-free recipes are wholesome and nutrient dense, yet delicious and incredibly satisfying. I'm so happy she has come out with another book of wonderful creations!"

~Elana Amsterdam
New York Times best-selling author of
Paleo Cooking from Elana's Pantry

"Maintaining proper health doesn't have to take up all of your time, even in today's fast-paced world. With *Make Ahead Paleo*, Tammy helps readers overcome modern-day obstacles to good health, such as busy schedules, frequent travel, and tight budgets, to make eating wholesome, nutrient-dense food incredibly easy. Thriving on the Paleo diet has never been easier!"

~Loren Cordain, Ph.D., Professor
author of *The Paleo Diet*

"This book will give you back the extra time you had when you still thought fast food was an acceptable part of your diet. Eating for peak health requires preparing the majority of your own meals, and Tammy Credicott delivers the help we all need to get more out of our time spent in the kitchen."

~Jason Seib
author of *The Paleo Coach*

"Planning ahead and being prepared is something I have preached for years, and thanks to *Make Ahead Paleo*, Tammy has given a guideline of preparedness so that you are ready for whatever might come your way. *Make Ahead Paleo* offers a surefire way to always have healthy meals for your family, even when traveling!"

~Sarah Fragoso
national best-selling author of
Everyday Paleo, Everyday Paleo Family Cookbook,
and *Everyday Paleo Around the World: Italian Cuisine*

contents...

Make & Freeze

Apple Ring
Pancakes

Breakfast Muffins

Paleo English
Muffins

Chocolate
Cinnamon Sweet
Potato Waffles

Sausage,
Onion & Tomato
Breakfast Quiche

Pizza Crust

Macadamia, Garlic
& Basil Crusted
Chicken

Mango Cilantro
Chicken

Pecan Stuffed
Chicken Thighs

Baked Turkey
Meatballs
with Sweet-n-Sour
Dipping Sauce

Apricot Orange
Pork Chops

Sausage Stuffed
Portobellos

Cowboy Burgers

Garlic Topped
Flank Steak
Roulade

Sloppy Joes

Cocoa Spice-
Rubbed Ribeyes

Creamy Beef
& Green Bean
Casserole
with Pearl Onions

Herb Marinated
Skirt Steak

Fajita Burgers

Smoky Fall Spice-
Rubbed Skirt
Steak

Pizza Pile

Low & Slow

Apple Cider Chicken Thighs

Asian BBQ Chicken

Coq au Vin

Jerk Chicken Legs

Slow Cooker Hunter's Chicken

Hula Chicken

Slow Cooker Chicken Tagine

White Chicken Chili

Thai Coconut Meatballs

5-Spice Pork with Scallions & Almonds

Blackberry Jalapeño Pork Roast

Maple Peach Pork Chops

Orange Sesame Ginger Pork Roast

Mushroom Meatballs

Bacon & Onion Roast

Flank Steak Rellenos

Ginger BBQ Beef

Chunky Chili Con Carne

Roasted Tomato Bacon Soup

Veggie Soup

On the Go

142
Cocoa Cinnamon Almonds

144
Ginger Orange Pecans

146
Paleo Party Mix

148
Nut-Free Granola Bars

150
Cracked Pepper and Chive Crackers

152
Cashew Lime Hummus

154
Sweet 'n' Smoky Deviled Eggs

156
Deviled Ham 'n' Eggs

158
Creamy Cilantro No Potato Salad

160
Jicama Carrot Slaw with Grilled Steak

162
Steak & Chard Salad with Roasted Beets

164
Tomato Avocado Salad with Grilled Chicken

166
Citrus Red Onion Slaw with Grilled Chicken

168
Grilled Chicken Antipasto Salad

170
Tomato Salad with Jalapeño Vinaigrette

172
Chicken & Egg Salad Stuffed Peppers

174
BLAST Sushi & Paleo Ranch Dressing

176
Thai Chicken Drumsticks

178
Best Ever Chicken Strips

180
Honey Mustard & Spicy Avocado Dipping Sauces

182
Shrimp Rolls with Nutty Ginger Sauce

Room Service

186

Br-Egg-Fast
Hot Dogs

188

Coffee Cup Eggs

190

Everything Skillet
Scramble

192

Pumpkin
Cardamom
Pancakes

194

Lemon Sage
Turkey Tenders

196

Cashew Lime
Chicken

198

Chicken with
Mushrooms and
Balsamic Cream
Sauce

200

Chicken Picatta
Bites

202

Chili Lime
Pork Medallions

204

Red Onion
Balsamic Pork Bites

206

Oregon Pork

208

Beef
with Snow Peas

210

Coffee Rubbed
Steak Strips

212

Ribeye Nuggets
with Jalapeño
Pesto

214

Red Curry
Steak Fajitas

Travel Treats

Almond
Shortbread
218

Chocolate Almond
Butter Swirls
220

Chocolate Dipped
Strawberry
Macaroons
222

Kitchen Sink
Cookies
224

Orange White
Chocolate
Macadamia Cookies
226

Lemon Blueberry
Coolers
228

Salted Chocolate
Cherry Jumbles
230

Almond Orange
Biscotti
232

No-Bake Sunbutter
Bars
234

Chocolate Chip
Tahini Blondies
with Toasted Coconut
236

Pumpkin Pie Bars
238

Cherry Pistachio
Scones
240

Elvis Muffins
242

Lemon Coconut
Loaf
244

Chocolate Chip
Banana Bread
with Cinnamon
Sugar Topping
246

Week in a Day

Sesame Chicken
Salad
254

Shredded Pork
Tacos with Mango
Salsa
256

Steak Cobb Salad
with Mango
Dressing
258

Bacon Chicken
Pizza
260

Pulled Pork
over Cauliflower
Rice with Spicy
Tomato Sauce
262

foreword...
by Sarah Fragoso

I've been living a Paleo lifestyle for more than five years. As I've regained my health, started the blog *Everyday Paleo*, and written two national best-sellers on the subject of Paleo, I've witnessed this grassroots movement turn mainstream almost overnight. As a result, I've observed thousands upon thousands of people return to a way of living that is not only sustainable but also produces results that are life-changing, to say the least. However, change as momentous as this is not always easy. Living in our modern world and trying to avoid processed convenience foods can be extremely challenging. As a busy mom, despite how much I preach preparedness and planning ahead, I still struggle to find the time to fit everything in. Eating real food means shopping, prepping, and cooking for my family, which I love to do, but to keep my sanity, resources like this book by Tammy Credicott are invaluable.

Make Ahead Paleo was written by a woman who lives a crazy life, just like you and I do. With kids and a husband and a career, Tammy knows firsthand how to make it all work—without excuses. Making a big change is often about changing your perspective, but it's also about changing your routine. Being prepared is something I have advocated for years, and in *Make Ahead Paleo*, Tammy gives guidelines for preparedness so that you can be ready for whatever might come your way. With this book, you're sure to always have healthy meals for your family, even when traveling! I especially love her *Room Service* section. I travel extensively, and staying Paleo can be the biggest challenge of being on the road. The best part of Tammy's book (besides the delicious recipes and handy tips) is that she helps families spend more time together, nurture relationships with loved ones, and be active doing things other than piles and piles of dishes. This is truly what living a Paleo lifestyle is all about—really living!

Tammy offers tons of tips on basics like how to properly freeze your meals for reheating and eating later. I've had a few freezer disasters myself, and wasted food is such a bummer, especially when you're counting on a fresh, tasty meal. Thankfully, Tammy takes the guesswork out of knowing which recipes are good for freezing and has included an entire section of *Make & Freeze* meals. Spend one day cooking and have a few days of dinners ready for those nights when an hour in the kitchen simply cannot be a part of the equation!

I also love Tammy's spice blends. How convenient and wonderful it is to have a quick meal ready to go with a spice blend that you have made yourself from ingredients you can trust. I won't give too much more away, but trust me, there are loads of other tips and tricks in this book—never mind the mouthwatering recipes that make this book a gem, and a must-have for your Paleo library.

thanks...

A very special and *huge* thank you goes out to every person who has checked out my website, purchased a book, found me on social media, or visited with me in person at events across the country! Without all of you, my *Healthy GF Life* fans, I wouldn't be able to continue my dream of helping others find happiness in the kitchen again, while tackling food allergies, health issues, and busy lifestyles. You have encouraged me from the very first gluten-free recipe I created and shared, and I can't thank you enough for your unwavering support. I am truly honored that you let me into your homes and kitchens. I hope I can continue to help and encourage you in some small way. Thank you!

Much gratitude goes out to Erich and Michele, the two leading members of my Victory Belt family. I can't tell you how enjoyable it is to work with the both of you! Collaborating with people you truly admire and have fun with is almost unheard of, so I count myself lucky every single day.

Thanks to Drea at Compliments Home Interiors in my hometown of Bend, Oregon. Not only are you amazingly talented, but you're also incredibly sweet. I can't thank you enough for finding me the gor-gee-ous kitchen where we shot some of my cover photos! And speaking of cover photos, thank you to Justin of Justin Earl Photography for taking a non-photogenic, camera-shy girl and not only making me feel comfortable, but also sneaking in some pretty good shots along the way. You have such a gift!

> "Laughter is brightest where food is best."
> – Irish Proverb

A special thank you to my mom for teaching me frugality in the kitchen; for loving your family enough to feed us well, no matter what was in the freezer; and for creating comfy recipes and time-saving shortcuts that kept good food on the table while allowing you to remain part of the family fun. I've had a great teacher and role model! And thank you to my sister, who took that upbringing and ran with it, showing me the peace of mind that comes with meal organization, planning, and sticking to a budget. That means I must also thank those whose bellies they feed—my dad, "bother"-in-law (hee hee!), niece, and nephew. Without your hungry mouths to feed, where would we be?

And of course, THANK YOU to my wonderful, patient husband and kids, who have put up with an inordinate amount of dirty dishes, failed recipes, and lack of a dining room (it's my photography studio). Thanks for sticking around through the chaos! While life gets really crazy in our household sometimes (okay, most of the time), we can't deny that we make a great team and have a lot of fun together. The three of you are my life's crowning achievements. I love you more each day and can't wait to tackle our next adventures!

P.S. – Thank you, Rilee, for stirring the sauce that one time. And thank you, Makenna, for taste-testing those cookies. What would I do without you two?

history...

Many of you may already know my story, my family's journey, and where we think we're headed. I say "think" because every day brings something new—some new bit of knowledge that ever so slightly (or sometimes violently and distinctly) pings us in a new direction.

Almost six years ago, the health and wellness path that my family and I had been wandering down changed direction abruptly over the course of only a few months. My husband was diagnosed with celiac disease, along with egg, dairy, and other miscellaneous food intolerances. My older daughter was having problems focusing in school, was diagnosed with ADD, and struggled with verbal communication and comprehension. At the same time, my younger daughter suffered from dermatitis, severe dark undereye circles, and night terrors. Ah, such good times. We were nowhere near the happy, healthy family I was promised. Oh, wait—there are no guarantees in life! My family members have always been the most important people in my world, but they were certainly making day-to-day life a challenge.

After the initial shock wore off from the news of my husband's diagnosis and the reality of what going gluten-free meant sank in, I actually felt grateful and relieved. Why? Because with my husband's celiac diagnosis came weeks of research on how to handle it. Our research turned up connection after connection between gluten, casein, artificial colors, etc. and the ailments my husband and kids were suffering from. We discovered that food was the central cause of all their health issues. (Cue the singing angels!) This was the game-changer; because the only thing worse than watching your family suffer from chronic health issues is not knowing what's causing them or how to fix them.

It quickly became evident that the only way for us to live our best life was to face this new way of eating head on. I felt that it was my job to make sure my family received as much nourishment as possible, both from food and from our family dynamic. I refused to let mealtime be something we avoided. I believed then, as I do now, that food is a tie that binds us all, and has for centuries. Food nourishes us, but it also provides time together for celebrating, sharing, and creating bonds. Now I just had to put it all into practice. But how?

I was pretty sure at that point that my meal ingredients would consist of air and water, since everything else seemed to be off-limits. So I did what I knew: the same ol' meal for me, a slightly adjusted meal for the kiddos to keep them happy [kids *must* eat (GF) mac-'n'-cheese, right?], and a *very* adjusted meal for my hubby. It took only one meal to figure out that this arrangement was not going to work for anyone. In addition to cross-contamination, all the extra work made me a very cross mom and wife! And no one is happy if mom isn't happy. I knew that in order

> "Food is our common ground, a universal experience."
> —James Beard

to keep everyone safe from possible cross-contamination—and from my mood—we'd all have to go gluten-free.

Prior to going gluten-free myself, I never once considered that *I* might have a food intolerance too. I mean, I didn't have skin issues. Those breakouts were just adult acne! I didn't have trouble digesting food either. All that gas, bloating, and weight gain were just the way my body worked. And the brain fog? Well, I wasn't 20 anymore. These things happen as we hit 29...okay, 30-something. Well, a week after going gluten-free, I had a nonstop headache, my stomach hurt, I was shaky, and I was hardly in the best mood. So I had a giant soft pretzel. I know, I know! Not the best choice. But at the time, I wasn't thinking clearly. All I knew was how badly I wanted and needed that pretzel! And I felt better within minutes of eating it. Great, even! That's when the realization hit that I'd been having withdrawal symptoms. Gluten was my drug, and I was detoxing. So gluten became enemy #1 in our household, and we were in this thing together—for good this time. No more soft pretzel binges!

On a gluten-free diet, my family saw positive results almost immediately. My husband's stomach felt better, and my older daughter's behavior and verbal skills improved. My younger daughter stopped having night terrors (which were actually triggered by dairy), her eczema cleared, and her dark undereye circles faded. Although I didn't see such dramatic changes in myself, the frequent headaches I'd had in the past did stop. Of course, I couldn't be sure whether the improvement was a result of avoiding gluten or the fact that my family was feeling better and was no longer so...well, demanding.

After our initial success, I wrote my first

> "Let food be thy medicine and medicine be thy food."
> —HIPPOCRATES

book, *The Healthy Gluten-Free Life.* I wrote it as a transitional tool for those wanting to step away from the typical gluten-free version of the Standard American Diet (SAD), which is lacking in nutrients and loaded with sugar, toward a healthier gluten-free life. And though *The Healthy Gluten-Free Life* is not entirely free of sugar and grains, it's a world away from what is currently the norm in the gluten-free community. The journey to health and good eating is incremental for most people, and *The Healthy Gluten-Free Life* offers assistance with that first step in the right direction.

Fast-forward a couple of years, past a short experiment with veganism. All the while we were eating a diet consisting of 80% gluten-free grains and sugar. I realized that while everyone felt *better* on a gluten-free diet, no one was feeling *great*. My husband was still having frequent stomach ailments, and while my kids' issues were much less severe, there was still a lot of room for improvement. And myself? (It always comes back to me, doesn't it?) I was still overweight, tired, and cranky. I thought this gluten-free thing was supposed to make everything perfect!

Then my husband found Paleo. (Cue the singing angels again, please!) Almost immediately, he started to gain back healthy weight, and his previously ashen face returned to its normal color. I decided that I needed to support his efforts and give the diet a try, so I read about the Paleo lifestyle and jumped in with both feet. My first week

was rocky, to say the least. Even though I'd been gluten-free for quite a while, I soon realized how heavily I'd relied on gluten-free grains and sugar as the bulk of my daily diet. That first week, my body literally ached for more grains—a quick fix for my plummeting blood sugar. But after a week or so, I lost five pounds, my skin cleared up, and I regained the kind of mental clarity I'd forgotten was possible. I haven't looked back since, and I can honestly say that I haven't felt this good in twenty years. Over the course of about seven months, I lost almost thirty pounds and went down three clothing sizes! Plus, I sleep more soundly and wake up ready to tackle my days—something that had eluded me for almost a decade.

> "All you need is love. But a little chocolate now and then doesn't hurt."
> – Charles M. Schulz

I then wrote my second book, *Paleo Indulgences*, which is a great bridge from a gluten-free life to a Paleo diet. In it, I provide recipes that can help folks stay on track by offering better choices for occasional treats that are still Paleo-friendly. Our modern world is very social, and social interaction inevitably involves food. We attend barbecues, birthday parties, and school functions—sometimes on a daily basis, it seems. Socializing is as important to our overall well-being as the food we eat and the amount of sleep we get. *Paleo Indulgences* was designed to help people enjoy gathering with friends and family while staying on track nutritionally.

I know that keeping up with work, school, social activities, and other obligations while providing quality meals for your family isn't easy. That's why I take shortcuts in the kitchen to make every minute count. With this book, I am passing along some of the tricks and techniques that I use to manage our busy lives. These techniques can help you continue to eat well without spending every waking moment standing in the checkout line or slaving over the stove.

Our modern world is a busy one. To be our best physically, mentally, and emotionally, and to be able to keep up with whatever comes our way, we must take care of ourselves. And food is where it all begins. So no matter what the TV ads try to sell you or the media tries to convince you, health and happiness cannot be found in a drive-thru or a prepackaged dinner. When you ignore what goes into your mouth, you choose to be unhealthy, uncomfortable, and unhappy. To take control of your health and, therefore, your life, you *must* start in the kitchen. You *must* cook in order to eat the best foods. Period!

> "Get people back into the kitchen and combat the trend toward processed food and fast food."
> – Andrew Weil

It's time to put you, your family, your health, and your happiness at the top of the priority list again. And it begins at home. My hope is that in some small way, this book will help you make your way back to the kitchen. If you're already comfortable cooking, I hope that it saves you time and gives you more freedom to have fun and connect with those you love. Now let's make some food!

"Man seeks to change the foods available in nature to suit his tastes, thereby putting an end to the very essence of life contained in them."

-SAI BABA

what is paleo?

Living a Paleo lifestyle means eating foods that our bodies recognize as food—foods that are as close to their natural state as possible. It means eating foods that were generally available to our hunter-gatherer ancestors, not processed and packaged in a laboratory. You've heard people say, "If your grandmother wouldn't recognize it, don't eat it!" Pretty good advice. Unfortunately, though, our food has been adulterated for centuries, and looking to Grandma just doesn't go back far enough.

{ "Food is your body's fuel.
Without fuel,
your body wants
to shut down."
-KEN HILL }

Here are some basic guidelines for eating Paleo:

☑ Enjoy grass-fed, pastured meats and wild-caught fish and seafood.

☑ Enjoy healthy, natural fats such as coconut oil, avocado, tallow, lard, and duck fat.

☑ Enjoy lots of organic veggies.

☑ Enjoy organic fruits, but not too many.

☑ Enjoy nuts and seeds in moderation.

☑ Avoid grains, legumes, soy, vegetable oils, refined sugars, artificial colors and sweeteners, and highly processed foods.

☑ Consume grass-fed dairy in moderation and only if your body can tolerate it. It's best to avoid dairy if you have an autoimmune disease or are trying to lose weight.

☑ Use natural sweeteners such as raw, organic honey, pure, organic maple syrup, coconut nectar, coconut sugar (also known as coconut crystals or palm sugar), and maple sugar in moderation. It's best to avoid sweeteners if you're trying to lose weight.

{ "Not eating meat is a decision,
eating meat is an instinct."
-DENIS LEARY }

If you are just starting to learn about this whole Paleo thing, I encourage you to research beyond the basic principles I've outlined here. In order to fully appreciate the journey you're about to begin, it is vitally important that you learn the science—the "why"—behind the Paleo diet and really understand what modern foods do inside the body. Without knowing the "why" of Paleo, it will be just another diet that feels restrictive. You must want to eat to be healthy, not to be a size two!

There is an abundance of great information available to help you learn more about the Paleo lifestyle. Read, read, and read some more. Knowledge is power when it comes to your body and your health. Don't go through life knowing more about the functions of your iPhone than about the functions of your body. Here are some places to start:

Robb Wolf – Check out his *New York Times* best-selling book, *The Paleo Solution*. In it he presents the science of the diet with a sense of humor and in terms that are easy to understand and apply.
www.robbwolf.com

Mark Sisson – Mark's book, *The Primal Blueprint*, gives you the step-by-step guidance you need when you ask yourself, "Where do I start?" His laid-back style is contagious and will give you a whole new appreciation for learning to be a kid again.
www.marksdailyapple.com

Sarah Fragoso – Sarah is the queen of positivity and support in the Paleo community. Her books, *Everyday Paleo*, *Everyday Paleo Family Cookbook*, *Everyday Paleo Around the World Italian Cuisine*, and *Paleo Pals* (for kids), are full of great advice, information, and recipes. Check out her websites for tons of information and articles that will motivate you quickly.
www.everydaypaleo.com and
www.eplifefit.com

Jason Seib – Make sure to read Jason's book, *The Paleo Coach*, for the most uplifting stories and real-world motivation you'll find in the Paleo-sphere. You'll laugh out loud while you race to set up an appointment at your nearest gym. He also teamed up with Sarah Fragoso to form Everyday Paleo Lifestyle and Fitness.
www.eplifefit.com

Diane Sanfilippo – Diane is the author of *Practical Paleo*, a wonderful get-started guide for everyone, especially those with autoimmune diseases. It contains lots of great, easy-to-read information with meal plans and recipes.
www.balancedbites.com

Nora Gedgaudas – Nora is the author of *Primal Body, Primal Mind*, in which she goes in depth as to what those processed carbs are really doing inside your body and, more importantly, your brain.
www.primalbody-primalmind.com

Paleo Magazine - *Paleo Magazine* is the first and only print magazine dedicated to the Paleo lifestyle and ancestral health. This bimonthly publication is packed with the latest research, exercises, recipes, and nutrition information.
www.paleomagonline.com

{ "The only time to eat diet food is while you're waiting for the steak to cook." }
-JULIA CHILD

it isn't just about the food...

The thing I love most about Paleo is that it isn't just a diet, but a lifestyle. I know, I know, you've heard that before, right? But it truly is! Absorb yourself in the Paleo community long enough, and first you'll hear a lot about food, which is what makes you feel amazing initially. But then you'll see that it's really about simplifying your life to make time for food and family, reducing stress, sleeping well in a dark room (not with the neighbor's porch light glaring in your face), lifting heavy things (properly), and playing. Yes, *playing*! And the best part is, you get to do it all the time. Every day! Not just for the first few weeks, and then go right back to your stressed, sleep-deprived self.

{ "One should eat to live, not live to eat."
-MOLIERE }

A healthy life is comprised of many factors, not just food. But if you start with food, you'll be willing and able to address the other areas of your life that are making you unhealthy and unhappy.

and this works in the modern world how?

How does Paleo work in the modern world, you ask? By simplifying, simplifying, simplifying! Our world is stressful and hectic because, when it comes down to it, we *choose* for it to be that way. We choose the stressful job. Or we choose to stay in the stressful job because we have chosen the nice car and the too-big house. We choose to do ten million activities for the family, and we choose what groceries we buy and what we stuff into our mouths.

So what's the first step? *Choose* to simplify! From reducing work hours to decluttering your home, choose to take away the layers that don't matter so that you can get to the gooey, delicious center of life—the good stuff like playing with your kids, cooking a meal together, or having dinner outside on a blanket and not in front of the TV. You'll be amazed at the feeling of weight being lifted off of your shoulders when you choose to simplify.

{ "Sharing food with another human being is an intimate act that should not be indulged in lightly."
- M. F. K. FISHER }

Get back to the basics by:

{ Doing a job you enjoy and not working excessive hours. }

{ Taking time for *you* regularly. }

{ Taking time to have some fun with your spouse regularly. }

{ Reconnecting with the positive people in your life. }

{ Cooking and eating meals together as a family each and every night. }

{ Reading more
Turn off the TV and read a book together. My kids love to read books that my husband and I enjoyed as kids. You'll have a ball reacquainting yourself with childhood characters you've long forgotten. }

{ Playing!
Running around with your kids, riding bikes, playing on the jungle gym, skating—anything you can do together. Your kids will love seeing you smile and have fun! }

{ Going on adventures!
Weekend or day trips are great ways to get out of the house, step away from electronics, and really enjoy one another. Find places in your area that you've never bothered to check out before. Make sure to take along snacks and meals from *Make Ahead Paleo!* }

"Maybe a person's time would be as well spent raising food as raising money to buy food."

-Frank A. Clark

getting the family aboard the paleo train...

Just by implementing the changes I've already talked about, your family will be more open to changing their diet. Once your spouse and kids see you having fun spending time with them and playing, they'll want to be a part of whatever made you so happy and energetic! But here are a few extra tips that can help crack the tough nuts:

☑ ***First and foremost, stop labeling your meals as "breakfast," "lunch," "snacks," etc.*** Labels create unnecessary boundaries in the creative process of meal planning. If you call it breakfast, all you can think of is toast and cereal. Call it a snack, and you want foods that are typically unhealthy and come in crinkly packages. These definitions have been taught to us over our lifetimes by TV programming and the food industry; it's not that our bodies want or need certain foods at certain times of day. Who says you can't have a steak or salmon in the morning or bacon at night? Once you let go of labels, the preconceived notions of "what foods we eat when" disappear, and you simply have *meals* again. One of my favorite time-savers is to put a roast in the slow cooker before I go to bed so that we have a delicious meal ready when we wake up. Say goodbye to labels and hello to feeling full and satisfied by eating the right foods no matter what time of day it is!

> { "Family is not an important thing. It's everything."
> -MICHAEL J. FOX }

☑ ***Paleo-ize the foods your family already loves.*** Some people need to know that they aren't giving up a special food forever, and that's okay. If you make Paleo brownies, cookies, and pizza so that your family can give up drive-thrus and plastic-packaged food-like items, go for it. Using the *Travel Treats* recipes in this book, as well as recipes from my previous book, *Paleo Indulgences,* can make the transition much easier. Eventually, you can start reducing the amount of Paleo treats they eat, but for now, do whatever it takes to get them on board.

☑ ***Phase out one food at a time, if necessary, to lessen the shock.*** No one said that you have to do it cold turkey! Do make sure that, at some point, you give strict Paleo 30 days to feel the full positive effects. In the beginning, though, feel free to remove one food at a time until you've Paleo-ized your kitchen.

☑ ***Tell them the doctor said so.*** I know it's a little sneaky, but do whatever it takes to get your family to take Paleo seriously. Some spouses and kids are more apt to listen to authority than a loved one. If no one is listening, bring in the big guns.

☑ ***Don't tell them at all!*** I know many moms who simply started making Paleo meals. It's really not hard; just eliminate the pasta or rice and serve an extra veggie. Add some delicious Paleo treats, and your family will never know the difference. Well, not until they start feeling better and losing weight!

☑ ***Kids are more willing to jump on board if the decision is theirs and they help.*** Read to them about it, and talk *a lot* about their bodies and how foods make them feel. Kids don't want to feel bad either! You'll be surprised at how quickly they start regulating their own choices once they know how the chocolate milk at school is making them feel. Then have them help plan their school lunches, snacks, and even some dinners. Let them make a grocery list with you (I used picture lists for my little ones when they weren't reading/writing yet), shop with you, and help you cook. Kids are much more likely to eat and enjoy what they've helped to prepare. Buy kid-sized kitchen tools such as scissors for cutting up veggies and herbs and smaller spatulas that they can handle easily and safely. They can even learn to cut with small knives that aren't too sharp.

> "All great change in America begins at the dinner table."
> -RONALD REAGAN

☑ ***Keep ready-to-eat snacks within easy reach.*** I like to keep washed, cut-up veggies in mason jars in the door of the refrigerator. My kids go to town on veggies without being asked because it's their choice to eat them whenever they want.

☑ ***Buy cool lunch containers—not just for the kids, but for you too.*** You'll need to keep healthy foods handy as you run errands, so buy a Thermos and an insulated lunch carrier to keep in the car. Some of my favorites are:

Laptop Lunches: www.laptoplunches.com

LunchBots: www.lunchbots.com

Thermos: www.thermos.com

Hydro Flask: www.hydroflask.com

> "Some of the most important conversations I've ever had occurred at my family's dinner table."
> -BOB EHRLICH

stocking your paleo kitchen...

When buying pantry items, look for organic products in BPA-free cans or glass containers. This list isn't all-inclusive by any means, but it's a great place to start in turning your SAD kitchen into a Paleo powerhouse! You can find where to buy many of these items in the resource section on page 265.

Pantry:

- ☑ almond flour (not meal)
- ☑ arrowroot starch
- ☑ baking powder
- ☑ baking soda
- ☑ cocoa powder
- ☑ coconut butter
- ☑ coconut flour
- ☑ coconut milk (full fat with no carrageenan)
- ☑ coconut oil, virgin (tastes like coconut) and refined (doesn't taste like coconut)
- ☑ nuts and seeds
- ☑ olive oil
- ☑ parchment paper
- ☑ pure almond extract
- ☑ pure maple syrup
- ☑ pure vanilla extract
- ☑ raw honey
- ☑ tapioca starch
- ☑ tomatoes (diced, paste, sauce)
- ☑ tuna, salmon, crab, etc.
- ☑ vinegars (balsamic, coconut, raw apple cider, red wine, white wine)

Spice rack:

- ☑ allspice
- ☑ basil
- ☑ bay leaves
- ☑ black peppercorns (buy a grinder)
- ☑ cardamom
- ☑ chili powder
- ☑ chipotle chili powder
- ☑ cinnamon
- ☑ coriander
- ☑ cumin
- ☑ dill
- ☑ granulated garlic
- ☑ granulated onion
- ☑ ground mustard
- ☑ Italian seasoning
- ☑ marjoram
- ☑ nutmeg
- ☑ oregano
- ☑ paprika
- ☑ rosemary (ground)
- ☑ sea salt (Celtic, pink Himalayan, Real Salt)
- ☑ smoked paprika
- ☑ thyme
- ☑ turmeric

Refrigerator:

- ☑ coconut aminos
- ☑ duck fat
- ☑ farm-fresh eggs
- ☑ fermented foods (kraut, kimchee, etc.)
- ☑ fish sauce
- ☑ fish and seafood
- ☑ fruits
- ☑ ghee
- ☑ lard
- ☑ meats
- ☑ tallow
- ☑ vegetables

> "One cannot think well, love well, sleep well, if one has not dined well."
>
> -Virginia Woolf, *A Room of One's Own*

stand-ins...

The first time you try a recipe, I recommend that you make it as-is, with no substitutions of any kind, so you know what the end result should be. If you change multiple ingredients, the recipe is no longer the same, and the result may be less than great. Of course, once you're comfortable with a recipe, I encourage you to play and tweak the ingredients to suit your tastes.

Dairy:

The recipes in this book do not call for dairy ingredients, but if you prefer, you can use butter in place of coconut oil with good but varying results. For example, cookies may spread more if you use butter. In place of coconut milk, you can use full-fat, unpasteurized, organic milk or unsweetened almond milk if you prefer.

Eggs:

Because ingredients in Paleo baking are so minimal and contain no gluten from wheat flour or gums used in traditional gluten-free baking, I don't yet have a simple replacement for eggs. As I discover new solutions, I will add them to my website, www.thehealthygflife.com, so be sure to check back often. With experimentation I have found some success replacing eggs with a flax "gel" or applesauce in certain recipes. I have noted the substitution in the ingredient list in those recipes.

Fats:

Most of my recipes use coconut oil, but some call for olive oil or organic palm shortening. You can substitute walnut oil or butter for the coconut oil or olive oil, and butter for the palm shortening with good, but slightly varying, results.

Flour:

For recipes using almond flour, you can substitute another finely ground nut or seed flour, but not almond meal. I often use finely ground raw sunflower seeds as a replacement for almond flour with exceptional results. But keep in mind that alternative flours must be very finely ground, which generally can be achieved only commercially or in a high-speed blender such as a VitaMix or BlendTec. Replacing a finely ground almond flour with a coarse flour or meal will not yield the same results. You can see the difference between the two in the photos on the next page.

Sweeteners:

I use pure organic maple syrup in most of my recipes because I love the flavor and the fact that it's lower in fructose than honey. However, I use raw, organic honey occasionally, and it's a great substitution. Studies say that the fructose in honey may be metabolized differently in our bodies than processed fructose such as high-fructose corn syrup. For any of the recipes in this book, you can use pure maple syrup, raw, organic honey, and coconut nectar interchangeably. In recipes that call for coconut sugar (also known as palm sugar or coconut crystals), the dry form, you can substitute maple sugar.

Almond Flour

Blanched Almond Meal

budget control...

One of the first things folks say about Paleo is, "It's so expensive!" I don't argue that your grocery bill may inch up initially, especially when you compare the cost of a bag of chips to the cost of a steak. But when you factor in all the food-like items that you stop buying (chips, cupcakes, ice cream, packaged and drive-thru meals, milk, bread, soda, etc.) and factor in your future reduced medical bills, it really does even out. And I know it's hard to believe, but once the family is eating Paleo, you will actually eat less in a day than on the traditional SAD (standard American diet). Quality foods like grass-fed meat, good fats, and veggies will keep you fuller longer so that you aren't eating constantly throughout the day.

{ "Food
is an important part
of a balanced diet."
- FRAN LEBOWITZ }

Here are some additional ways to save money in the checkout line:

Buy meat in large quantities. Buying meat in value packs is cheaper per pound than making smaller purchases. Just separate the meat into meal-sized portions when you get home, and freeze what you won't use right away.

Use the bulk bins! You know those funny-looking clear containers you always walk by in the health food store? Stop ignoring them, because they are filled with savings! Purchasing nuts, seeds, dried fruits, dried unsweetened coconut, and even spices in bulk can save you tons of cash. Just be careful if you have a severe food allergy or celiac disease, as cross-contamination can be an issue in this area of the store.

Check out online deals. One would think that purchasing food online for delivery to your door would cost more, but you'd be surprised at the values you can find on the web! If you have trouble finding grass-fed meats or other quality ingredients, great deals are only a click away. Companies such as US Wellness Meats, Lava Lake Lamb, and Fat Works offer periodic discount codes and occasional free shipping deals that make their prices very affordable. You can find a list of some of my favorite online companies in the resource section (page 264).

Find a CSA (community supported agriculture) in your area. With a CSA, a farmer offers a certain number of shares to the public. Your share typically gets you a bag or box of produce at specific times, such as once a week, throughout the farm's growing season. These boxes contain anything from lettuce to eggs to berries; the mix varies depending on your region and what's in season. This is a great way to buy local, seasonal food directly from a farmer at great prices. Check out the resource section (page 265) to find a CSA near you.

Visit local farms or connect with them at farmer's markets. Some smaller farms that don't offer CSA shares still welcome consumers to purchase produce directly from their farmstands. The resource section (page 265) lists websites to help you find farms in your area.

Of course, use *Make Ahead Paleo* every week to help you prepare meals in advance and save money by not wasting ingredients!

{ "You're not going to reform the way we farm and process food unless you cook." }
-MICHAEL POLLAN

my kitchen philosophy...

Real, quality ingredients are at the heart of my recipes. You can assume that throughout the book, I want you to:

☑ *Choose organic whenever possible.*

☑ *Choose meats from animals that lived the way nature intended.* This means organic, grass-fed, pastured, or wild-caught. Meats such as bacon and sausage should be uncured and free of added nitrites and nitrates.

☑ *Whenever I refer to lemon juice or lime juice, I always mean fresh squeezed.*

☑ *In all recipes, eggs are always large.*

☑ *Maple syrup means real, organic maple syrup, not corn syrup in a squeeze bottle.*

☑ *Vanilla extract means real, organic, pure vanilla extract with no sugar added.* Anything called "vanillin" or "imitation vanilla" should never enter your shopping cart or home. Ever.

☑ *Use raw, organic, local honey whenever possible.* The flavor and nutrients are far superior to the clear, processed honey that comes in a bear-shaped bottle.

☑ *Condiments such as ketchup and mayo are a gray area for my family because we just don't use them frequently enough to make our own.* For us, it makes sense to purchase the highest quality condiments we can find. Look for organic versions with no soy or sugar added. If I can't find a sugar-free version of something like Worcestershire sauce, I don't stress, because the tiny amounts I use here and there aren't going to ruin my efforts. When I do take the time to make my own mayo and ketchup, I use Sarah Fragoso's fantastic recipes from her cookbook *Everyday Paleo* and on her website, www.everydaypaleo.com, or the mayo recipe from the talented Michelle Tam of www.nomnompaleo.com.

☑ *Coconut should be unsweetened and dehydrated.* I use two kinds: finely shredded and larger coconut flakes.

> "When I eat with my friends, it is a moment of real pleasure, when I really enjoy my life."
> -Monica Bellucci

☑ ***Dark chocolate should be 85% cocoa or higher and free of soy and dairy.*** That said, this type of chocolate can be difficult to find, and it is less than economical to use a $5 chocolate bar in a cookie recipe. For those times, I love Enjoy Life brand mini chocolate chips and chocolate chunks. While the sugar content is higher than in an 85% dark chocolate bar, these chocolate pieces are free of gluten, dairy, and soy. I've also been known to combine a chopped 85% dark chocolate bar with some mini chocolate chips to help them go further and reduce the sugar a bit.

> "The most remarkable thing about my mother is that for thirty years she served the family nothing but leftovers. The original meal has never been found."
>
> -CALVIN TRILLIN

I view recipes as a base—a jumping-off point to create your own meals and flavors. Use the recipes in this book, and once you're comfortable, adjust them to your family's tastes. Get creative! Find inspiration in other cookbooks and on the Internet. Take regular recipes and ask yourself what you can change to make them allergy- and Paleo-friendly.

To be honest, I'm a lazy cook. I need meals that are quick, simple, flavorful, and made with real food. I don't like to spend hours in the kitchen because I'd rather be out playing, and I'm sure you feel the same way. So I developed a system that keeps dinners on the table and a smile on my face (most of the time, anyway!).

My secret lies in the three Ps:

Planning
– Make a weekly or monthly menu

By planning ahead and jotting down your menu for the week or even the month, you know what to buy and what to take out of the freezer. Plus, you avoid the most dreaded question of all, "What's for dinner?" The choice to hit a drive-thru, order a pizza, or eat a bag of chips for dinner takes place in the after-work, 5:00 p.m. window when you're tired and hungry and can't think of anything to make. Planning a menu keeps you out of this danger zone. You will know what's for dinner each and every day, and best of all, you'll have the ingredients in your home to make it!

Purchasing
– Buy the food

I know this sounds easy enough, but you have to actually make a grocery list from your menu and shop for the ingredients. The food will not magically show up on your doorstep. Believe me, I've waited for the grocery fairy, and she never, ever comes. By setting aside an hour each week, you can make your grocery list (based on your menu, of course) and purchase everything you need at the store in less time than it takes to watch an episode of *American Idol*.

Preparing
– Spend some time here and there prepping ingredients

How much extra time does it take to chop two onions instead of one? Thirty seconds? This is just one of the tricks I use to keep my freezer stocked with ingredients I can throw together at a moment's notice. Making double batches of sauces, cooking twice the meat needed, and freezing the extras are all great ways to have a freezer full of ready-to-go fixings. And by using the recipes and methods in this book, you'll always have great food at the ready!

nutritional info...

I don't include nutritional information in my recipes or books, first and foremost because I don't believe in measuring, weighing, and calculating every crumb that goes into my mouth. I believe that real, quality foods should be enjoyed not only for flavor, but also because they provide nutrients for the body. In general, if you're consuming Paleo foods, you don't need to worry about the nutritional breakdown of your meals. Eat until you're satisfied and then stop.

If you're really concerned about the foods you're eating, you need to be honest with yourself. You probably shouldn't be eating them in the first place, or you should be eating them in very small amounts. A treat is a treat and should be handled as such.

Finally, I'm not a dietician or a nutritionist. It would be irresponsible of me to provide that information without the background to do it properly. If you truly want to calculate your total calorie intake, there are many excellent food journals on the web that can help you.

{ "Too many people just eat to consume calories. Try dining for a change." -JOHN WALTERS }

"It's easy
for Americans to forget
that the food they eat
doesn't magically appear
on a supermarket shelf."
-CHRISTOPHER DODD

use every trick
in the book (literally)...

Make-Ahead
Tips & Tricks

Plan your make-ahead and freeze prep days based on common ingredients. For example, if chicken thighs are on sale, buy a bunch and plan to make all your chicken recipes in a single afternoon.

Planning and shopping for your make-ahead menus one day and doing the prep cooking the next day is easier on you than doing it all in one day.

Be sure to clean as you go! On prep day, fill the sink with hot, soapy water and clean as you cook so that you aren't faced with a pile of dirty dishes at the end. ☺

Label everything that goes into the freezer clearly so that you can identify it easily.

Whenever you chop veggies such as carrots, onions, peppers, celery, leeks, broccoli, and cauliflower, cut extra. Chopping a few more doesn't take much more time. Freeze the extras in 1- or 2-cup portions to make them easy to pull out when you need them later in the month.

The same goes for meat. When you're grilling chicken, throw on a few extra pieces for leftovers the next day, or cool and freeze them for later use.

❄ ❄ ❄

Whenever you make a sauce to serve with your protein, double it. Use half that night, and freeze the other half for later. Soon you'll have a freezer full of go-to sauces that you can just thaw, heat, and serve.

 Precook breakfast meats like bacon and homemade sausage patties. Cooking them at the beginning of the week and refrigerating them for midweek breakfasts saves a lot of time. Just heat and eat!

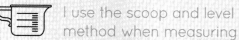 I use the scoop and level method when measuring flour. This means dipping the measuring cup into the flour container, scooping the flour into the cup, and then leveling by running the straightedge of a butter knife over the top. I am not freakishly accurate here. If there's a lump or two that is technically higher than the edge of the measuring cup, it's okay. Just don't level so low that you scoop out some of the flour below the cup edge. I'd rather you have slightly too much flour than not enough. Why? Because it's oh-so-easy to add extra liquid to a recipe that's a little dry because of too much flour. On the other hand, once you add all the liquid to a recipe, you can't take it out again if it's too runny because of not enough flour.

When measuring coconut flour, measure the amount the recipe calls for using the scoop and level method, and then dump it into a sifter (over your mixing bowl) and sift.

If a recipe calls for "coconut oil, melted," it means to measure first and then melt. I've found that measuring after melting and melting after measuring gives you pretty much the same result, but for baking recipes, I measure before melting. If it's summer, of course, it doesn't matter because the oil will already be in liquid form.

Don't overcrowd the pan! I'm frequently asked, "Why didn't my meat brown nicely like in the photo?" The answer is overcrowding in the pan. Piling meat into a skillet creates steam, which prevents meats from browning properly. The trick is not to let the pieces of meat touch each other when you put them in the pan, even if it means cooking the meat in batches.

Another common mistake is not cooking in a hot enough pan. The secret to a good sear or caramelized veggie (apart from avoiding overcrowding) is a hot pan. Putting food into a hot pan also prevents sticking. A good way to know whether your pan is hot enough is to check that the oil has little ripples in it. Oil that isn't hot enough just looks clear.

The third trick to a good browning of ingredients is not to turn food too early or often. Set the meat in the skillet and don't touch it! No matter how badly you want to lift it up after a minute, don't. Wait a couple of minutes and then lift the meat gently. If it doesn't come up easily, it isn't ready to be turned. Once it is seared, it will lift easily for flipping. I *promise*.

Be sure to give meat a ten-minute rest after cooking before you slice it. Doing so will ensure that the juices stay where they belong. Cutting immediately after cooking releases the juices all over the cutting board and leaves you with dry meat. Not good.

Doubling the coconut flour in a recipe doesn't yield the proper results. There's no magic formula, but www.marksdailyapple.com gives a good guideline for substituting and doubling coconut flour in recipes. I generally use slightly less than double the amount of coconut flour, and adjust the liquids as needed. For example, if a recipe calls for ¼ cup coconut flour (doubled would be ½ cup), I would bring it down to ⅓ cup or even ¼ cup plus 1 or 2 tablespoons when doubling. It's always better to err on the side of not quite enough coconut flour than too much.

Always, always use parchment paper for baking. With Paleo ingredients, baked goods will usually spread flat as pancakes if baked directly on a baking sheet. Parchment paper helps baked goods hold their shape, promotes nice brown bottoms, and makes for easy cleanup. Look for unbleached parchment paper at health food stores.

For optimal flavor, use fresh herbs when called for. In a pinch, though, dried herbs can replace fresh. Remember that you need much less of a dried herb because the flavors are more concentrated.

Precook a few sweet potatoes at the beginning of the week. Peel, dice, toss in coconut oil, and oven-roast them at 450°F for twenty minutes or until they are soft but firm and not mushy. Refrigerate them until needed on a busy morning (which is pretty much every morning in our house).

Short on time? Cut meats such as chicken, pork, and beef into bite-sized chunks to speed cooking time. I don't advise using this method for grilling meats, however. Just trust me on that one.

Find a favorite spice blend and keep it on hand for quick seasoning. Here are my go-to blends:

Taco Seasoning

In a jar with a tight-fitting lid, combine:

- 2 TBSP chili powder
- 1 ½ TBSP paprika
- 1 TBSP cumin
- 1 TBSP granulated onion
- 2 ½ tsp granulated garlic
- 2 tsp sea salt
- Pinch of cayenne

Use 1 ½ TBSP of taco seasoning plus ¼ cup of water for every pound of meat. Simmer for 5 minutes.

Italian Seasoning

In a jar with a tight-fitting lid, combine:

- 2 TBSP basil
- 2 TBSP marjoram
- 2 TBSP oregano
- 1 TBSP rosemary (ground)
- 2 tsp thyme
- 2 tsp granulated onion
- 2 tsp granulated garlic

Use to season meat or fish, or sprinkle on salads.

Dry Rub

In a jar with a tight-fitting lid, combine:

- 1 TBSP granulated onion
- 2 tsp granulated garlic
- 2 tsp sea salt
- 1 tsp black pepper
- 1 tsp paprika
- 1 tsp marjoram
- ½ tsp basil
- 1 tsp dried parsley
- 1 tsp dry mustard
- ¼ tsp ground rosemary
- ¼ tsp smoked paprika
- ¼ tsp oregano
- ⅛ tsp cumin

Sprinkle on steaks, chicken, or even sweet potatoes before cooking.

Miscellaneous
Tips & Tricks

Most meals will consist of a protein and two types of veggies. Serve one veggie raw, like pepper slices or cucumber spears. Doing so saves kitchen time because you have to cook only the meat and one vegetable.

Be sure to measure ingredients in the proper vessel. Liquid measuring cups are for, you guessed it, liquids! Dry measuring cups are for dry ingredients like almond flour. Measuring spoons are for smaller, incremental measuring. Don't measure dry ingredients in a liquid measuring cup; it won't yield accurate results.

Chop onions, peppers, and carrots once a week and freeze them in small portions in zip-top bags. Use them as quick add-ins for stir-fry, slow cooker meals, etc.

Don't waste a thing! Freeze "leftovers" like asparagus ends and leek ends in a zip-top bag and use them when you need to increase the flavor and nutrient profile of stock.

If you use a fresh lemon for zest and don't need the juice, squeeze the juice anyway and freeze it in ice cube trays. When you need lemon juice for a sauce, just add a cube, or melt it first in the microwave.

The easiest way to peel ginger is with a small spoon. Just scrape the peel right off while keeping your knuckles intact. Keep peeled ginger pieces in the freezer. Frozen ginger lasts longer and is easier to grate.

Freeze leftover coconut milk in ¼-cup portions to use later without needing to measure again. Just thaw it first because coconut milk ice cubes don't work well with hand mixers.

Don't throw those brown bananas in the trash! Freeze them in zip-top bags to add to smoothies or use in banana bread recipes. Frozen and thawed overripe bananas are the best-kept secret to moist, flavorful banana bread.

Handy Kitchen Tools

- ☑ Cooling racks
- ☑ Digital meat thermometer
- ☑ Electric skillet (they make many sizes and even stainless steel ones if you don't want nonstick)
- ☑ English muffin rings
- ☑ Food processor
- ☑ Glasslock food containers (www.glasslockusa.com)
- ☑ Good-quality mixing bowls in various sizes

- ☑ Hand mixer
- ☑ High-speed blender
- ☑ Immersion blender
- ☑ Kitchen scissors (about four pairs; you'll need every one)
- ☑ Magic Bullet Blender (the perfect size for salad dressings)
- ☑ Mason jars with lids
- ☑ Parchment paper (unbleached)
- ☑ Scoops

- ☑ Sheet pans
- ☑ Sifter
- ☑ Slow cooker
- ☑ Small chest freezer
- ☑ Storage containers (see the resource section on page 265)
- ☑ Tongs, both short and long
- ☑ Two sets of measuring spoons and cups
- ☑ Zester

Kid-Sized Equipment

🙂 Get a hand-operated food chopper (like the Pampered Chef version), and small hands can help you chop veggies without the risk of cutting fingers.

🙂 Keep a pair of extra-long tongs on hand for kids to help stir, flip, or toss without getting too close to hot stoves and pans.

🙂 Keep a pair of kid-safe scissors in a kitchen drawer. Little ones can use them to safely cut green onions and herbs like basil leaves, parsley, cilantro, and chives.

🙂 Keep a wooden meat tenderizer mallet for pounding chicken breasts or other cuts of meat flat. A wooden one is easier to handle and much lighter than its metal counterparts, and kiddos love smashing things!

🙂 Get a few pieces of kid-sized cooking equipment. Purchasing one extra small frying pan and a small spatula just for the kids will give them the confidence to handle the tools safely.

about the book...

In *Make Ahead Paleo*, I've included recipes that cover many approaches to "making ahead." I utilize all these methods at home depending on where we're headed on trips or what the month looks like. I tried to keep the ingredients simple and utilize meats that are easy to find at most grocery stores and tend to go on sale frequently, including beef, chicken, and pork. For this reason, I didn't include fish or many shellfish recipes, and I left out other types of harder-to-find meats and wild game.

Make & Freeze

The first section, *Make & Freeze*, contains make-ahead-and-freeze recipes that you can easily create in a few hours here and there. You can whip up one or two portions or spend the afternoon making four or five batches of the same recipe to fill up the freezer. This is a great way to use bulk meat purchases and know that you always have an entrée ready to go...just thaw and cook! I've also found this method handy for camping trips. I simply prep and freeze everything, and as it thaws in the cooler, I cook it up! Also included in this section are some items that you can prebake and thaw to enjoy when you're ready.

What to Store	Pantry/Countertop	In Fridge	In Freezer	Freezer How-To
Grapes	no	1 to 2 weeks	8 to 12 months	Wash & pat dry. Spread on tray & freeze until firm. Store in a sealed freezer bag.
Bananas	5 days	2 weeks	8 to 12 months	Peel first. Store 4 bananas per freezer bag for easier measuring.
Berries	no	2 to 7 days	8 to 12 months	Wash and pat dry. Spread on tray & freeze until firm. Store in a sealed freezer bag.
Apples	3 to 4 days	up to 4 months depending on variety	8 to 12 months	Core, peel, slice, & toss in lemon juice to prevent browning. Spread on tray & freeze until firm. Store in a sealed freezer bag.
Cherries	no	3 days	8 to 12 months	Wash, dry and pit. Spread on tray & freeze until firm. Store in a sealed freezer bag.
Melons	3 to 4 days	5 days whole; 3 days cut	6 to 12 months	Cube or slice without rind. Spread on a tray & freeze until firm. Store in a sealed freezer bag.
Peaches/ Plums/ Nectarines	1 to 2 days	5 days	6 to 12 months	Peel, remove pit & slice. Place on a tray & freeze until firm. Store in a sealed freezer bag.
Peppers	no	1 week (green); 5 days (red, yellow, orange)	6 to 9 months	Wash, chop or slice & store in a sealed freezer bag.
Onions	2 months	4 days (cut)	3 to 6 months	Peel, chop & store in a sealed freezer bag.
Sweet Potatoes	2 weeks	3 days (peeled, diced)	2 to 3 months	Peel, dice & store in a sealed freezer bag. Store cooked, cooled and mashed sweet potatoes in airtight containers.
Tomatoes	3 to 4 days	no	no	no
Most Other Veggies	no	1 to 7 days	3 to 6 months	Most veggies like broccoli & cauliflower freeze well after blanching, cooling & drying. Spread on a tray & freeze until firm. Store in a sealed freezer bag.
Steak	no	3 days	6 months	Store in freezer bags.
Chops	no	3 days	6 months	Store in freezer bags.
Roasts	no	3 days	6 months	Store in freezer bags.
Ground	no	2 days	4 months	Store in freezer bags.
Bacon	no	2 weeks (unopened); 1 week (opened)	1 month	Store in original packaging placed inside a freezer bag.
Sausage, raw	no	2 days	2 months	Store in freezer bags.
Fish	no	2 days	6 months	Store in freezer bags.
Shellfish	no	2 days	3 to 4 months	Store in freezer bags.
Poultry	no	2 days	4 to 6 months	Store in freezer bags.

FRUITS

VEGGIES

MEATS/SEAFOOD

What to Store	Pantry/Countertop	In Fridge	In Freezer	Freezer How-To
Quick Breads (muffins/pancakes)	no	3 to 4 days	2 to 3 months	Store in freezer bags or airtight container.
Yeast Breads	no	1 to 2 days	3 to 6 months	Store in freezer bags or airtight container.
Coconut Flour	no	6 months	12 months	Store in freezer bags or airtight container.
Almond Flour	no	6 months	12 to 18 months	Store in freezer bags or airtight container.
Starches	1 to 2 months	6 to 8 months	12 to 18 months	Store in freezer bags or airtight container.
Cookies	2 to 3 days	1 week	3 months	Store in freezer bags or airtight container.
Coconut Milk, canned	2 to 3 years (unopened), use by exp. date on can	7 - 10 days in a separate container	3 to 6 months in an a separate container	Store in an airtight container. Leave room at the top for expansion when it freezes.
Ghee	6 months (unopened)	9 to 12 months	12 to 18 months	Store in original container.
Butter, sticks	no	3 months	6 months	Store in original packaging placed inside a freezer bag.
Broth, homemade	no	7 days	3 months	Store in an airtight container. Leave room at the top for expansion when it freezes.
Nuts/Seeds	1 month	6 to 12 months	1 to 2 years	Shell first. Store in an airtight container or freezer bag.
Coconut, shredded	6 months (unopened)	8 to 12 months	12 to 18 months	Store in freezer bags.
Dried Fruits	6 months (unopened)	no	no	no

BAKING

MISC

Freezing Tips

Prepare meals in assembly-line fashion. Making three or four portions of the same meal is super-easy if you line up your containers and fill each one as you work through the recipe. This is why I didn't include double or triple batches. It's much faster and easier to measure one recipe per container than doubling a batch and dividing between two containers.

* * *

Remove as much air as possible from bags and containers before placing them in the freezer. Air is the enemy of fresh food! The more air you remove, the fresher your food stays.

* * *

Always cool cooked foods completely before freezing. Freezing warm foods causes ice crystals to form inside the containers, resulting in soggy meals.

* * *

Choose the right containers. I like to use a few 1-quart and 2-quart containers as holders for my freezer bags as I fill them. Doing so keeps them standing upright and helps avoid spills. Make sure to purchase zip-top bags made specifically for the freezer, as they are thicker and keep food safer longer. If you're using glass containers, make sure they have a tight seal. My go-to containers are Glasslock, mason jars, and zip-top freezer bags. See the resource section on page 265 for more information.

* * *

Be sure to label every container or bag before it goes into the freezer! You may think that you'll remember what's what, but three months from now, all that frozen food will look the same.

* * *

Thaw freezer meals in the refrigerator, usually overnight. If your refrigerator runs on the colder side, it may take two days, so be sure to plan accordingly. I like to remove items from my freezer on Sunday for meals Monday through Wednesday. On Wednesday I remove the meals I need for the remainder of the week.

* * *

Keep your freezer organized by storing like items together. In a stand-up freezer, you can use shallow bins, and in a large chest freezer you can use boxes or crates. I organize my freezer by meat and cut. For example, all the ground beef is together, while all the pork chops are in a separate container.

* * *

Blanching most veggies, like broccoli and cauliflower, prior to freezing is an important step because it stops the enzyme action that can cause them to lose flavor, color, and texture. It also removes any surface bacteria. To blanch veggies, place them in boiling water. When the water returns to a boil, continue boiling them for two to three minutes. Remove the veggies with a slotted spoon and place them in a bowl of ice water to stop the cooking process. Drain them completely, pat them dry, and place in freezer containers.

* * *

Keep an inventory of your frozen creations so that you don't freeze your fingers off when you try to find what you want. You can use the tear-out freezer inventory sheets in the back of the book (and print more from my website, www.thehealthygflife.com), or you can post a dry-erase board by your freezer and update it as you put in or take out items.

* * *

Low & Slow

The next section is a collection of slow cooker recipes that will truly save your sanity. In *Low & Slow*, with a little prep in the morning, your delicious dinner will be waiting for you at the end of a long day!

The unique combination of locked-in moisture, low cooking temperature, and longer cooking time makes the slow cooker a great no-fuss, no-worry, busy cook's best friend. Most slow cookers range in size from 1 to 7 quarts. The size you choose is important and depends on your needs. I recommend that a typical family of four own two slow cookers. I know that they're kitchen storage hogs, but they truly are indispensable time-savers and worth the extra space. I own and frequently use 4-quart and 6-quart slow cookers. I use the larger one for bone broth and one-pot meals, including large roasts and whole chickens, when I'm also adding veggies that take up a lot of space. I use the 4-quart cooker when I'm cooking a smaller amount of meat that wouldn't fill the larger cooker. Now, I don't do this because I hate the pathetic look

of a lonely pork tenderloin in the bottom of a cavernous pot. I use both sizes because, for the best results, the slow cooker container should be one-half to three-quarters full. Not filling the cooker sufficiently will likely result in burned or overcooked food, while overfilling can result in undercooked food, which isn't good for anyone.

Most slow cooker recipes offer both a low and high setting option. It's important to know how long you want your meals to cook so that you aren't staring at a shrunken, dehydrated roast at the end of the day. You don't want to set your cooker to high, thinking you'll eat in four hours, but then let it cook for eight hours while you run errands.

Slow cookers are designed to cook in the "gentle simmer" range, so the difference in appliance settings lies in how fast your slow cooker reaches cooking temperature. It will reach this point faster on high than on low. According to most slow cooker manufacturers, you can use the following as a guide:

Low (175-185°F): 7-8 hours of cooking

High (200-212°F): 3-5 hours of cooking

Another important point, which many often forget, is not to lift the lid of your slow cooker a million times during the cooking process. I know it's hard, but just trust that it's working and leave the lid on! A vacuum seal is created during cooking that helps your meal cook properly for the right amount of time and stay moist. Of course, if you're toward the end of the allotted cooking time and you feel that your meal may be done, by all means check it to avoid overcooking. But early on, lifting the lid reduces the cooking temperature, and getting it back up to speed can take anywhere from twenty to thirty minutes, affecting your total cooking time.

In many recipes, I recommend browning meats before placing them in your slow cooker. This is, by all means, optional. I prefer the look and flavor of browned meats, so I almost always take this extra step. But I understand that a busy weekday morning sometimes warrants a "dump and run" approach. You will still have a tasty meal at the end of the day; it just won't look quite as pretty or have quite the depth of flavor that browning provides. But do what you need to do, because taking the step of having a healthy meal, no matter what it looks like, is much more important than not cooking it at all just because you couldn't brown the meat first.

On the Go

If your family is like mine, you do a lot of traveling. Whether it's an all-day adventure or a weeklong vacation, you'll need portable fare that doesn't disintegrate in the cooler. Plus, nothing passes the drive time like easy-to-eat car snacks, and nothing keeps the show tunes humming along like a good pit stop with picnic edibles. With the recipes in my *On the Go* section, you'll hit the road well fed!

Here are some additional travel tips that we use when taking off:

Flying has become a little trickier because of the rules and regulations you'll face at the security gate. The biggest things to remember when packing snacks in that carry-on are:

☑ Each liquid or gel can be in a 3.4-ounce (100ml) bottle or less (by volume).

☑ All liquid containers must fit nicely inside a 1-quart, clear plastic, zip-top bag. I've found that different brands offer different dimensions, so buy a few to see what works for you.

☑ Each passenger can bring only one zip-top bag through security.

So what does this mean for the weary Paleo traveler? Pack your own snacks, buy water after you go through security, and hope like heck that your flights aren't delayed! After many trips with and without kiddos, I've compiled my own list of snacks and tips for flying without succumbing to the food-like items that they sell in most airports:

✈ **If you're bringing anything that needs to stay cold, be careful.** While cold gel packs are allowed for breast milk and medicines, I've gotten no straight answer as to whether they're allowed for food. Most airports say no, and many of my bags have been taken at security, even when they were under the 3.4-ounce limit. A better option is to take along two extra zip-top bags and ask one of the food vendors for a few ice cubes after you go through security. Seal the bag, wrap it in a few napkins, and stick that bundle in the second zip-top bag. This creates an ice pack with a buffer for leaks and condensation. If you have to travel through a security checkpoint again, simply dump the water and repeat the process.

✈ **Bring along a small (3.4-ounce or less) bottle of olive oil and a small container of sea salt,** available at health food stores or online, to dress salads purchased from airport food vendors. A lot of places can safely grill a piece of chicken and prepare a salad with nothing on it. Just drizzle on your oil and a sprinkle of sea salt, and voilà! You have a Paleo meal on the go.

✈ **Take along foods that can handle a beating in your carry-on.** Be sure to pack them in sturdy, non-glass containers. Check out the resource section (page 264) for information on where to find some of these travel snacks. Here are some foods you can take with you:

- *Jerky*
- *Epic bars*
- *Chomps Snack Sticks*
- *Dried fruit*
- *Nuts/seeds*
- *Sandwiches made on Paleo English Muffins (page 60)*
- *Homemade nut and fruit bars*
- *Dark chocolate squares*
- *Homemade granola*
- *Cheese and Paleo crackers*
- *Fruits (apple slices with cinnamon sprinkled on top, orange slices, frozen grapes, strawberries)*
- *Veggies (carrot sticks, celery sticks, grape tomatoes, cucumber slices)*
- *Breakfast Muffins (page 58)*

 *On the Road*

While a few of the recipes in my *On the Go* section will work well in a carry-on, most are geared toward road trips or for the cooler once you arrive at your destination. Here are some of our other favorite take-along snacks and some of our tried-and-true travel tips:

✓ All the foods mentioned for flying work well on the road too.

✓ If I'm craving something fizzy to wash away the road dust, I opt for a sparkling water with lemon slices.

✓ To keep from getting drowsy, try munching on organic sunflower seeds. Be sure to bring a cup for the shells.

✓ Boiled eggs are the perfect portable protein source.

✓ Other great on-the-go proteins are beef jerky, canned salmon, tuna, and sardines.

✓ I like to bring a small container of ghee and coconut oil so that I have healthy fats at the ready.

✓ Travel with a cooler, of course! Bring food that you've prepared at home from *Make Ahead Paleo*, and store any produce purchases you find along the way.

✓ Be sure to investigate local health food stores and farmer's markets at your destination. You'll be making gourmet meals in your kitchenette with the wholesome ingredients you can find. Plus, it's a great way to sample local fare, which adds to the enjoyment of your vacation. You can find information about how to locate farmer's markets on page 265.

✓ When planning your trip, be sure to book a hotel with a kitchenette. They usually cost a little more, but you'll save more than the difference by preparing just one meal in your room rather than eating at a restaurant.

✓ Google your destination for restaurants that provide quality food. You'll be surprised by how many places are popping up that serve local, grass-fed meats and offer gluten-free menus.

✓ Always plan extra time on your route for a picnic. Bring a blanket, plates, and utensils so that you can picnic anytime, anywhere.

✓ Check out meal delivery businesses at your destination. I've been to cities such as San Francisco, Los Angeles, and Miami, and all have Paleo meal delivery businesses. Before you leave, order meals to be delivered to your hotel. These businesses are usually very accommodating and friendly!

✓ Order frozen meals online and have them shipped to your hotel. There's a wonderful company called Artisan Bistro (www.artisanbistropro.com/pc530473) that makes allergy-friendly Paleo meals that you can order online. Just heat them in your in-room microwave!

Room Service

Of course, you'll need a plan for meals once you arrive at your destination, so I've included a handy *Room Service* section with meals that you can easily make in your hotel room. Sure, you can Paleo-ize many restaurant meals, but you still get an overabundance of rancid vegetable oils and questionable-quality meats.

With my *Room Service* recipes, you will spend a little time at home preparing ingredients and placing them in individual containers such as mason jars or Glasslock, but it will minimize messes and speed up cooking time in your room. Plus, they pack nicely in a cooler. Throw in an electric skillet, use your in-room microwave, and you're set to create quick and virtually mess-free meals in the comfort of your hotel room! Of course, please double-check with the hotel to confirm that it allows portable appliances, and always cook with care. Don't forget the essential supplies: electric skillet, spatula, splatter screen, salt, pepper, towel, travel dish soap, sponge, plates, napkins, and utensils.

Travel Treats

Considering the busy lives of families today, there's never a shortage of reasons to have a supply of Paleo goody recipes that travel well. I've included a section of tasty *Travel Treats* so that you can bring amazing indulgences to soccer games, school parties, and that upcoming office party you've been dreading. For baked goods, remember that you can make your own dry mixes at home! Simply combine the dry ingredients a recipe calls for in an airtight container and store it in the fridge until needed. You'll want to bring the mix to room temperature before proceeding with the rest of the recipe directions.

Cocoa Spice-Rubbed Ribeyes

- 4 ribeye steaks
- 1 TBSP Italian seasoning
- 2 tsp granulated onion
- 1 tsp granulated garlic
- 1 tsp paprika
- ½ tsp cumin
- 1 tsp chili powder
- 2 tsp cocoa powder
- ½ tsp sea salt
- Freshly ground black pepper to taste
- 1 TBSP honey
- 3 TBSP very strong brewed coffee

Serves 4

These steaks are hearty, have rich and satisfying flavors, and are easy to make. But this recipe wasn't planned. It was a by-chance happening one day as I spun around in a circle in my kitchen, grabbing different ingredients. You never know when the results will be fantastic, so I suggest taking the time to experiment with spices every so often. You just might end up with a winner!

Prep Day:

1. Place the steaks in a 1-gallon freezer bag.

2. In a small bowl, combine the Italian seasoning, granulated onion, granulated garlic, paprika, cumin, chili powder, cocoa powder, sea salt, and pepper.

3. Sprinkle the mixed spices over the steaks in the bag.

4. Drizzle the steaks with the honey and coffee. Remove the air from the bag, and squish the steaks around to coat them.

5. Store the bag in the freezer until needed.

Serving Day:

1. Thaw the steaks in the refrigerator overnight.

2. When ready to cook, fire up your grill to medium-high heat. When the grill is hot, cook the steaks to medium, about 4 minutes per side, depending on their thickness.

3. Let the steaks rest for 10 minutes before serving.

Creamy Beef & Green Bean Casserole with Pearl Onions

BEEF INGREDIENTS

- 2 TBSP coconut oil
- ⅓ cup chopped yellow onion
- 1½ pounds ground beef
- 2 cloves garlic, minced
- Sea salt to taste
- Freshly ground black pepper to taste

SAUCE INGREDIENTS

- 1 TBSP coconut oil
- 8 ounces white button mushrooms, sliced
- 1 cup chicken broth
- Sea salt to taste
- Freshly ground black pepper to taste
- 1 TBSP arrowroot starch
- ¾ cup coconut milk

ADD-INS

- 1 pound frozen green beans
- 1 cup pearl onions (outer skins removed)

FOR SERVING DAY

- 3 TBSP coconut oil
- 3 large shallots, thinly sliced

Serves 4

This casserole brings back memories not only of Thanksgiving green bean casserole, but also of a lovely little dish that my mom used to make called Tater Tot Casserole. Remember it? I know that many of you do! It had tater tots, canned mushroom soup, and ground beef and was the only way my mom could get me to eat green beans! I was not a veggie lover as a kid. I was an "earth-toned eater," my parents used to say. Since then, I've gotten over my veggie-phobia and created this gussied-up version of the classic with the addition of pearl onions and fried shallots, making it a modern-day comfort food. The crispy shallots really make this dish, so be sure to cook plenty!

Prep Day:

1. In a large skillet over medium heat, melt 2 TBSP coconut oil.
2. Add the onion, and sauté until softened, about 3 minutes.
3. Add the ground beef, garlic, sea salt, and pepper. Brown the beef, stirring occasionally, for 6 minutes.
4. Transfer the beef mixture to a large bowl, and set it aside.
5. To make the sauce, add 1 TBSP coconut oil to the same skillet.
6. Add the mushrooms, and cook them until they are browned and the liquid has evaporated, about 8 minutes, stirring occasionally.
7. Turn up the heat to medium-high, and slowly whisk in the chicken broth, making sure to scrape the delectable brown bits off the bottom of the pan.
8. Add sea salt and pepper, and bring the mixture to a simmer for 1 minute.
9. In a small bowl, whisk the arrowroot starch into the coconut milk. Slowly add this mixture to the simmering broth, whisking as you pour it in.
10. Bring the liquid just to a simmer, and remove the pan from the heat.
11. In the large bowl with the beef, add the sauce, green beans, and pearl onions. Stir to combine.
12. Place the entire mixture in a 2-quart casserole dish, cover it, and refrigerate it to let it cool completely.
13. Once cooled, seal the dish with a lid or plastic wrap. If using plastic wrap, also cover it with foil, and freeze until needed.

Serving Day:

1. Thaw the casserole in the refrigerator overnight.

2. When ready to cook, preheat your oven to 350°F.

3. Remove the plastic lid or wrap and foil, and re-cover the dish with a fresh piece of foil. Bake for 45-55 minutes or until bubbly.

4. Meanwhile, in a large skillet, heat 3 TBSP coconut oil over medium heat.

5. Add the shallots to the skillet, stirring to coat them in the oil. Cook without stirring until they start to turn golden brown, about 3-4 minutes.

6. Stir the shallots, and continue to cook, stirring occasionally, until all the pieces are golden brown. Transfer the shallots to a paper towel-lined plate, and sprinkle them with sea salt.

7. Spread the crispy shallots evenly over the top of the casserole, and serve.

Herb Marinated Skirt Steak

STEAK

- 2 pounds skirt steak, cut into thirds

MARINADE

- ⅓ cup olive oil
- 3 TBSP coconut aminos
- ¼ cup lime juice
- ¼ cup tomato sauce
- 3 TBSP honey
- 2 green onions, sliced
- 2 cloves garlic, minced
- 1 small shallot, minced
- 1 TBSP chopped fresh rosemary
- 2 tsp chopped fresh thyme
- 1 TBSP chopped fresh oregano
- ¼ cup chopped fresh parsley
- ¼ cup chopped fresh basil

Serves 4

My family loves the tender, juicy flavor of skirt steak, but this yummy marinade goes well with just about any cut of beef. From tri-tip to flank steak or even poured over a roast in the slow cooker, this marinade will fast become one of your go-to recipes. The fresh herbs are the star of the show here, so be sure not to take a shortcut and use dried. It just wouldn't be the same.

Prep Day:

1. Place the skirt steak in a 1-gallon freezer bag.

2. In a small bowl, mix together the marinade ingredients.

3. Pour the marinade over the steak pieces in the bag. Remove the air from the bag, and seal. Squish the bag gently to coat the steak in the marinade.

4. Place the bag in another 1-gallon freezer bag. Remove the air, seal, and freeze until needed.

Serving Day:

1. Thaw the steak in the refrigerator overnight.

2. When ready to cook, heat the grill to medium-high heat.

3. Remove the steak from the freezer bag, and discard the bag and leftover marinade.

4. Grill the steaks for 3 minutes per side or until they are cooked but still pink in the center.

5. Transfer the steaks to a platter, tent with foil, and let them rest for 10 minutes.

6. Slice the steak against the grain, and serve.

Fajita Burgers

- 1 TBSP coconut oil
- ¼ cup diced red onion
- ⅓ cup diced red bell pepper
- ⅓ cup diced green bell pepper
- 2 pounds ground beef
- 1 egg (or 1 TBSP ground flax seeds mixed with 3 TBSP hot water; let it sit for a few minutes until it gels)
- 2 TBSP chopped fresh cilantro
- 1 clove garlic, minced
- ¼ tsp cumin
- 1 tsp chili powder
- ½ tsp paprika
- ½ tsp granulated onion
- ¼ tsp granulated garlic
- ½ tsp sea salt
- ¼ tsp freshly ground black pepper

makes 6 burgers

I love the flavor of fajitas: grilled steak, peppers, and onions...mmm! So I decided to throw those bold flavors into a burger one evening, and wow! Easy to prep ahead and freeze, these burgers will be ready anytime you want a classic burger with a zesty twist. I love topping these off with my favorite hot sauce; thank goodness there are lots of great gluten-free options available now!

Prep Day:

1. In a large skillet over medium heat, melt the coconut oil.
2. Add the onion and peppers, and sauté, stirring occasionally, for 3 minutes or until softened. Set them aside to cool.
3. In a large bowl, place the ground beef, egg, cilantro, garlic, cumin, chili powder, paprika, granulated onion, granulated garlic, sea salt, and pepper.
4. When the onion and peppers are cool enough to handle, spoon them into the bowl with the beef mixture.
5. Mix the beef and veggies gently with your hands to combine all the ingredients.
6. Divide the meat mixture into 6 equal parts, and shape them into patties with your hands.
7. Line a baking sheet with wax paper. Place the patties on the wax paper, making sure that they don't touch one another. Place the baking sheet in the freezer.
8. When the burger patties are semi-frozen, place them in a freezer bag with small pieces of wax paper separating them, and freeze until needed.

Serving Day:

1. Remove either the whole bag or one patty at a time from the freezer, and allow the burger(s) to thaw in the refrigerator overnight.
2. When ready to cook, fire up your grill to medium-high heat.
3. Grill the burger(s) for 4 minutes per side or until they have reached the desired doneness.

Smoky Fall Spice-Rubbed Skirt Steak

RUB INGREDIENTS

- ½ tsp sea salt
- ¼ tsp freshly ground black pepper
- 1 tsp smoked paprika
- 1 tsp dry mustard
- ½ tsp cumin
- 1 tsp coriander
- ½ tsp granulated garlic
- 2 tsp granulated onion
- ½ tsp turmeric
- ½ tsp chili powder
- 1 tsp allspice
- ¾ tsp rosemary
- ¾ tsp cinnamon

STEAK

- 2 pounds skirt steak
- 2 TBSP honey

Serves 4

When fall rolls around, this spice-packed skirt steak will keep you full and satisfied. I can't get enough of the smoky flavor and end up making this standby meal often during the cooler months. My favorite part, aside from the great taste, is that we get a filling, healthy meal that doesn't take much time to make!

Prep Day:

1. Place the rub ingredients in a small bowl, and stir to combine.

2. Cut the skirt steak into thirds so it's easier to handle on the grill. Sprinkle the rub mixture on all sides of the steak pieces. Really rub it in with your hands to distribute it evenly. Place the meat in a large zip-top bag.

3. Drizzle the honey into the bag, push out all the air, and seal. Now squish the meat around in the bag and get the honey all over the pieces. Place this bag inside a 1-gallon freezer bag and freeze until needed.

Serving Day:

1. Thaw the steaks in the refrigerator overnight. Remove the steaks from the refrigerator and allow them to warm up to room temperature. Meanwhile, preheat your grill to medium-high heat.

2. Grill the steaks for 2-3 minutes per side for medium-rare. Remove from the heat to a warm plate, tent with foil, and let them rest for 10 minutes.

3. Slice the steaks against the grain, and serve.

Pizza Pile

PILE

- 1 medium spaghetti squash, cut in half lengthwise, seeds and pulp removed

SAUCE INGREDIENTS

- ¼ cup olive oil
- 1 small onion, diced
- 1 clove garlic, minced
- ¼ cup chopped fresh parsley
- 1 can (28-ounce) tomato sauce
- 2 cans (4-ounce) tomato paste
- 1 can (28-ounce) diced tomatoes
- ½ tsp oregano
- ½ tsp basil
- Pinch of rosemary
- 1 tsp sea salt
- Freshly ground black pepper to taste

TOPPINGS OF CHOICE

- Italian sausage
- Black olives
- Salami
- Pepperoni
- Diced onions
- Mushrooms
- Diced bell peppers

Serves 4

Prep Day:

1. Preheat your oven to 375°F.

2. In a glass baking dish, place the spaghetti squash halves cut-side down.

3. Fill the baking dish with water to about ½-inch up the sides of the squash.

4. Cover the pan with foil, and bake for 30-40 minutes or until softened.

5. Meanwhile, make the spaghetti sauce. In a large pot, heat the olive oil over medium heat.

6. Add the onion, and cook until soft, about 5 minutes.

7. Add the garlic and parsley, and stir to combine with the onion.

8. Add the tomato sauce, tomato paste, diced tomatoes, oregano, basil, rosemary, sea salt, and pepper. Stir to combine all the ingredients.

9. Reduce the heat to low, cover, and simmer for 30 minutes.

10. Remove the pan from the heat, let cool, and spoon the sauce into mason jars.

11. When the squash is done, remove it from the baking dish with tongs, and transfer it to a plate to cool.

12. Cook any toppings that need to be precooked, such as sausage, peppers, and mushrooms. When cool, place them in separate containers.

13. Separate the strands of spaghetti squash by running a fork from the stem end to the bottom of the squash, scraping as you go. Remove the loose strands, and place them in an airtight container.

14. Store the squash, sauce, and topping containers in the freezer until needed.

Serving Day:

1. Thaw the squash, sauce, and toppings in the refrigerator overnight.

2. When ready to cook, reheat the squash and toppings on the stovetop or in the microwave.

3. To assemble, place a spoonful of squash in a bowl and top it with spaghetti sauce and your favorite toppings. Enjoy the pizza flavor without the heavy crust!

My "bother-in-law," Tim, has a way with words and came up with the appetizing name for this dish. He's been in my life since I was about 12 because he and my sister were high school sweethearts. So he's like a brother, and, as he's led me to believe, brothers are bothers. My entire family has joined the Paleo community over the years, and we love using spaghetti squash as a base for many types of dishes. Once you load up your spaghetti squash with all the fixings, it's kind of just one big (tasty) pile—hence the name Pizza Pile. We also make a Taco Pile. It works. And, okay, I guess I kind of like my bother-in-law (but don't tell him I said that!).

Low & Slow

{ healthy dinners when you walk in the door! }

Apple Cider Chicken Thighs

CHICKEN INGREDIENTS

- 3 pounds chicken thighs, boneless or bone-in
- Sea salt to taste
- Freshly ground black pepper to taste
- 1 shallot, minced
- 3 cloves garlic, minced
- 1 Golden Delicious or Jonagold apple, peeled, cored, and sliced into ¼-inch pieces
- 1 bay leaf

SAUCE INGREDIENTS

- 1 cup apple cider
- ½ cup apple cider vinegar
- ¼ cup olive oil
- 1-2 tsp chopped fresh thyme (or ¼-1 tsp dried)

Serves 4

Fresh thyme works the best for this apple-y dish, but if you don't have any on hand, dried thyme will work too. Feel free to adjust this seasoning to your taste, as thyme has a distinct flavor and aroma. My family doesn't care for a strong kick of the spice, so I keep it to a minimum. You can add as much as 1 tsp of dried, however, if you love the flavor. The combination of apple cider and apple cider vinegar gives this chicken the powerful apple flavor I was looking for, which makes it a favorite dish in the fall months.

1. Place the chicken in a slow cooker, and season it with sea salt and pepper.

2. Sprinkle the shallot, garlic, sliced apple, and bay leaf over the chicken.

3. In a small bowl, mix together the sauce ingredients. Pour the sauce over the chicken.

4. Cook the chicken on low for 6-7 hours or on high for 4-6 hours.

5. Spoon the sauce over the chicken to serve. Or, if you're feeling adventurous, ladle some into a small pan and simmer it over medium heat until reduced by half, and then serve over the chicken. Doing so thickens the sauce nicely and concentrates the flavors.

Asian BBQ Chicken

CHICKEN

- 2 pounds boneless chicken thighs

SAUCE INGREDIENTS

- ⅓ cup coconut aminos
- ¼ cup tomato sauce
- 1 TBSP tomato paste
- 2 TBSP apple cider vinegar
- 1 TBSP fish sauce
- ⅓ cup honey
- 2 tsp sesame oil
- 2 cloves garlic, minced
- 1 shallot, minced
- 1 TBSP minced fresh ginger

GARNISH

- Sesame seeds
- Sliced green onions

Serves 4

This dish has turned into one of my personal favorite slow cooker recipes. I don't spend a lot of prep time getting ingredients into the slow cooker, and at the end of the day, the house smells amazing and dinner tastes just as good! If you're having one of those busy days, simply serve the chicken with the juices from the slow cooker. But if you're feeling a little "saucy," go for the option of reducing the cooking liquid into a taste explosion that really turns this chicken into something special!

1. Place the chicken thighs in the slow cooker.

2. In a medium-sized bowl, whisk together the sauce ingredients until fully combined. Pour the sauce over the chicken.

3. Cook the chicken on low for 6-8 hours or on high for 4-6 hours.

4. Serve it as is, or follow the remaining directions for a tastier sauce. Transfer the chicken from the slow cooker to a platter, and keep it warm by tenting it with foil.

5. Spoon the sauce from the slow cooker into a shallow pan, and bring it to a boil over medium heat. Reduce the heat to medium-low, and simmer the sauce until it is reduced by half, about 5-8 minutes.

6. Serve the reduced sauce over the chicken, and garnish with sesame seeds and sliced green onions.

Coq au Vin

- Whole chicken (4-5 pounds)
- Sea salt to taste
- Freshly ground black pepper to taste
- 2 tsp minced fresh thyme
- ½ tsp chopped fresh sage
- 1½ cups pearl onions, outer skins removed
- 1 cup sliced white button mushrooms
- 3 cloves garlic, minced
- 4 slices bacon, chopped, cooked until browned but not too crisp
- ⅓ cup red wine
- 1 cup chicken broth
- ¼ cup tomato paste

Serves 4

Coq au Vin is a traditional French dish that typically includes cut-up chicken, smoked meat, wine, and herbs. The chicken is braised to make it tender and delicious. I love taking the same flavors and throwing them into my slow cooker for a simple, no-fuss dinner that is tasty enough for company!

1. Place the chicken in a slow cooker. Remember to remove any unmentionables from the cavity first.

2. Sprinkle the chicken with the sea salt, pepper, thyme, and sage.

3. Place the onions, mushrooms, garlic, and bacon on and around the chicken.

4. In a small bowl, whisk together the red wine, chicken broth, and tomato paste. Pour the sauce over the chicken.

5. Cook the chicken on low for 6-8 hours or on high for 4-6 hours.

Jerk Chicken Legs

CHICKEN

- 3 pounds chicken legs

RUB INGREDIENTS

- 1 tsp allspice
- ½ tsp cinnamon
- ¾ tsp thyme
- ¼ tsp nutmeg
- 1 tsp granulated onion
- ¾ tsp granulated garlic
- 1 tsp sea salt
- ½ tsp freshly ground black pepper
- ½ tsp smoked paprika
- Pinch of cayenne
- 1 TBSP coconut sugar

SAUCE INGREDIENTS

- 1½ cups chicken broth
- 1 TBSP red wine vinegar
- 2 TBSP lime juice
- 1 TBSP tomato paste
- 2 cloves garlic, minced
- ¼ cup diced red onion
- 1 tsp red chili flakes

GARNISH

- Chopped green onions

Serves 4

The beautiful blend of spices in jerk seasoning is unique but perfectly balanced. You can vary the amount of each spice, however, to get the flavor that works for you. My family enjoys this version, mostly because I use only a pinch of cayenne so that the spice doesn't overpower their delicate palates. You can also control the heat by adding more or less cayenne and red pepper flakes. What's your spice threshold?

1. Place the chicken legs in a slow cooker.
2. In a small bowl, combine the rub ingredients.
3. Sprinkle the rub over the chicken legs. Using your hands, rub the seasoning over each leg. Then be sure to wash your hands with soap!
4. In a medium-sized bowl, combine the sauce ingredients.
5. Pour the sauce around the edges of the chicken legs in the slow cooker.
6. Cook the chicken on low for 5-6 hours or on high for 3-4 hours.
7. Serve the chicken with a few chopped green onions sprinkled on top.

Slow Cooker Hunter's Chicken

- 4-5 pounds chicken, whole or cut up
- Sea salt to taste
- Freshly ground black pepper to taste
- 2 cups cremini mushrooms, thinly sliced (about an 8-ounce package)
- 1 shallot, minced
- 4 cloves garlic, minced
- ½ cup white wine
- 2 cups chicken broth
- 2 cups chopped tomatoes (about 6 romas)
- 1 tsp chopped fresh tarragon (or ½ tsp dried)
- 1 TBSP chopped fresh parsley, plus more for garnish

Serves 4

Also known as Chicken Cacciatore (in Italian, cacciatore means "hunter"), traditional Hunter's Chicken is a braised chicken with tomatoes, onions, and herbs. Thanks to modern-day slow cookers, you don't have to tend to your chicken all day—yay! I like to use a whole bird for this recipe, but you can use a cut-up chicken if you prefer. Either way, I like to transfer it to a sheet pan after it cooks, cut it into pieces, and broil it in the oven to brown the skin. It's an extra step, but well worth the amazing flavor it provides. Also, on those nights you're feeling Martha-y (or Emeril-y, as the case may be), you can transfer some of the liquid from the slow cooker to a pan, add arrowroot starch to thicken it, and simmer. Delicioso!

1. Season the chicken with sea salt and pepper, and place it in a slow cooker.

2. Add the mushrooms, shallot, garlic, white wine, chicken broth, tomatoes, tarragon, and parsley to the slow cooker.

3. Cook the chicken on low for 6-8 hours or on high for 5-6 hours.

4. You can also cut the chicken into manageable pieces, and place it on a parchment-lined baking sheet. Broil it for 5-6 minutes or until the skin has browned.

5. Serve with additional chopped parsley.

Hula Chicken

CHICKEN
- 3 pounds chicken, cut into pieces, or chicken thighs (with bones and skin)

SAUCE INGREDIENTS
- ¾ cup coconut aminos
- ¼ cup white wine
- ½ cup chicken or beef broth
- 2 TBSP honey
- ⅓ cup apple juice
- ½ cup chopped green onions

TOPPING INGREDIENTS
- ¼ cup honey, warmed slightly
- Chopped green onions
- Sesame seeds

Serves 4

I call this dish Hula Chicken because I want to do a little dance every time I eat it! It's hard to believe that such a short list of ingredients can deliver so much deliciousness. To keep things simple, you don't have to broil the chicken at the end, but doing so really adds to the texture and flavor of the dish, so I think it's worth the few extra minutes. Trust me; I wouldn't lead you astray!

1. Place the chicken pieces in a slow cooker.

2. In a small bowl, mix together the sauce ingredients.

3. Pour the sauce over the chicken, and cook on high for 4-5 hours.

4. Carefully remove the chicken pieces with tongs, and place them on a parchment lined-baking sheet.

5. Brush the chicken with the warmed honey.

6. Place the baking sheet under the broiler for about 5 minutes or until the chicken has browned and the skin is slightly crispy. Watch it carefully, as it can burn quickly!

7. Serve with chopped green onions and sesame seeds on top.

Slow Cooker Chicken Tagine

- 2½-3 pounds boneless, skinless chicken thighs
- 2 cloves garlic, minced
- 1 tsp chopped fresh thyme
- 1 tsp chopped fresh oregano
- 1 tsp sea salt
- Freshly ground black pepper to taste
- 1 lemon, thinly sliced
- ⅓ cup white wine
- 1 cup chicken broth
- ½ cup pitted, dried prunes, coarsely chopped
- ½ cup pitted, green olives, coarsely chopped
- 2 TBSP capers

Serves 4

This is chicken with a lot goin' on! Flavors come at you from all directions in this Moroccan-inspired dish, which is traditionally slow-cooked in a heavy clay pot called a tagine. In my kitchen, I throw all the ingredients in my slow cooker and let it do the work. Chicken has never tasted better with bright hints of lemon, sweet prunes, and the kick of capers and green olives!

1. Place the chicken thighs in a slow cooker.
2. Sprinkle the garlic, thyme, oregano, sea salt, and pepper over the chicken.
3. Place the lemon slices on and around the chicken.
4. Add the white wine, chicken broth, prunes, olives, and capers.
5. Cook the chicken on low for 5-6 hours or on high for 3-4 hours.
6. Serve the chicken with a spoonful of the juices and lots of the prunes, olives, and capers.

White Chicken Chili

CHILI

- 2 TBSP coconut oil
- 1 large onion, chopped
- 2 medium jalapeños, cored, seeded, and diced
- 4 cloves garlic, minced
- 1 tsp sea salt
- Freshly ground black pepper to taste
- 1 tsp cumin
- 1 tsp coriander
- ½ tsp chipotle chili powder
- 5 cups chicken broth
- Juice of 2 limes
- Zest of 1 lime
- 1½-2 pounds boneless, skinless chicken breasts, thighs, or both, cubed
- 1 can (4-ounce) chopped green chilies

GARNISH

- Chopped cilantro
- Diced avocado

Serves 4

This twist on traditional chili, made with chicken and broth instead of beef and tomatoes, is incredibly flavorful but quite simple to throw together in the slow cooker. If you like a thicker chili, you can add a little coconut flour or arrowroot starch during the last thirty minutes of cooking. My favorite trick, however, is to add some organic potato flakes to the pot. If you're okay with potatoes (evidence shows that they're filled with great nutrients), this is a super-easy way to thicken a sauce. And a small sprinkling of flakes will do! Try this with gravies too for a thick stock without any coconut flavor or the slimy texture that too much arrowroot starch can cause.

1. In a medium skillet, heat the coconut oil over medium-high heat.

2. Add the onion, jalapeños, and garlic, and cook, stirring occasionally, until softened, about 5 minutes.

3. Add the sea salt, pepper, cumin, coriander, and chipotle chili powder. Stir to combine, and cook for 1 minute longer.

4. Add the chicken broth, lime juice, lime zest, chicken pieces, and chilies to a slow cooker.

5. Add the cooked onion mixture over the top of the chicken mixture.

6. Cook the chili on low for 6-7 hours or on high for 4-5 hours.

7. To serve, pour the chili into bowls, and garnish each portion with chopped cilantro and diced avocado.

Thai Coconut Meatballs

MEATBALL INGREDIENTS

- 1 pound ground pork
- 1 pound ground turkey or beef
- 5 green onions, chopped
- 2 cloves garlic, minced
- 1 TBSP sesame oil
- 2 tsp fish sauce
- 1 TBSP coconut vinegar or apple cider vinegar
- 2 TBSP coconut oil

SAUCE INGREDIENTS

- 1 cup coconut milk
- ⅔ cup chicken broth
- ½-1 tsp red curry paste
- 1 TBSP pure maple syrup
- 1 TBSP lime juice
- 1 TBSP arrowroot starch
- 3 TBSP cold water

Makes 36 meatballs

Food that is fun and bite-sized is much more exciting to my kids than a big slab of meat. I'm not ashamed to say that I completely take advantage of this knowledge by making lots of "mini" dishes like mini-meatloaves, chicken bites, steak bites, and of course, meatballs. You'd be surprised what you can pack into a meatball without your kids knowing about it (liver and veggies are my favorite sneaky ingredients). But let's just keep that between us, okay? I left this meatball recipe pretty simple, though. I guess I wasn't feeling particularly sneaky that day. Still, they are delicious, and my kids can't get enough of the unique flavors. I hope your family loves them too!

1. In a large bowl, combine the pork, turkey or beef, green onions, garlic, sesame oil, fish sauce, and vinegar. Mix well with your hands, and form into 36 1½-inch meatballs.

2. In a large skillet, heat the coconut oil over medium heat.

3. Add the meatballs to the skillet, and cook, turning occasionally, to brown them on all sides.

4. Place the browned meatballs in a slow cooker. In a small bowl, combine the coconut milk, chicken broth, curry paste, and maple syrup. Pour over the meatballs.

5. Cook the meatballs on low for 5-6 hours or on high for 4-5 hours.

6. Add the lime juice, and stir gently.

7. In a small bowl, stir together the arrowroot starch and cold water. Add the mixture to the slow cooker, and stir gently.

8. Cook, uncovered, on high for 15 minutes, and serve.

5-Spice Pork with Scallions & Almonds

ROAST INGREDIENTS
- 4-5-pound pork roast
- Sea salt to taste
- Freshly ground black pepper to taste
- 3 TBSP coconut oil

SAUCE INGREDIENTS
- 3 cups chicken broth
- ¼ cup coconut aminos
- 2 cloves garlic, minced
- 1 tsp Chinese 5-Spice
- ¼ tsp freshly ground black pepper
- 2 green bell peppers, ribs and seeds discarded, sliced
- 1 yellow onion, sliced
- 3 scallions, sliced

GARNISH
- Sliced scallions
- ½ cup coarsely chopped roasted, salted almonds

Serves 4

I usually avoid buying spice blends because I figure I can make them myself a lot more economically. But Chinese 5-Spice is an exception. It's a blend of star anise, fennel, pepper, cinnamon, and cloves, and those bold flavors need just the right ratios. This fragrant blend, found in even the smallest grocery stores nowadays, adds a unique flavor to any Asian dish. And when you can get the full regional flavor of a dish with just a sprinkle of spices, it doesn't get any easier than that!

1. Season the pork roast with sea salt and pepper.
2. In a large skillet, heat the coconut oil over medium-high heat.
3. Place the pork in the skillet, and brown it on all sides.
4. Transfer the pork to a slow cooker.
5. In a small bowl, combine the chicken broth, coconut aminos, garlic, 5-Spice, and pepper. Pour the mixture over the pork.
6. Sprinkle the sliced peppers, onion, and scallions over the pork.
7. Cook on low for 6-7 hours or on high for 4-5 hours.
8. Using 2 forks, shred the pork while it is still in the slow cooker.
9. Serve the shredded pork with the sauce and veggies, garnished with sliced scallions and toasted almonds.

Blackberry Jalapeño Pork Roast

RUB INGREDIENTS

- 1 tsp sea salt
- ¼ tsp freshly ground black pepper
- 1 tsp granulated onion
- ¾ tsp granulated garlic
- ¾ tsp chili powder
- ½ tsp cinnamon
- Pinch of cayenne

ROAST INGREDIENTS

- 4-5-pound pork roast
- 3 TBSP coconut oil

SAUCE INGREDIENTS

- 1 cup apple juice
- 2 cups chicken broth
- 2 cups fresh or frozen blackberries
- 2 TBSP balsamic vinegar
- 3 cloves garlic, minced
- ½ medium yellow onion, chopped
- 2 jalapeños, stems removed, sliced
- ½ tsp red chili flakes

Serves 4

This sweet and spicy roast will keep you full and warm on those gray winter days! The blackberries get sweeter as they cook, and with the addition of some heat from a few jalapeños, the unique combination of flavors really hits the spot. If you like your food a little less spicy, you can tame the flame by removing the seeds and ribs of the jalapeños before slicing and adding them to the slow cooker. I like this dish with just a touch of spice, so I add a few slices of jalapeño with seeds and ribs and scrape the rest clean. You still get the wonderful jalapeño flavor with just a little bit of kick!

1. In a small bowl, combine the rub ingredients.
2. Sprinkle the rub over the pork roast, and rub it with your fingers to thoroughly coat all sides of the meat.
3. In a large skillet, heat the coconut oil over medium-high heat.
4. Place the roast in the skillet and brown on all sides, about 8 minutes.
5. Transfer the roast to a slow cooker.
6. In a medium-sized bowl, combine the sauce ingredients.
7. Pour the sauce over the roast in the slow cooker, and cook on low for 6-7 hours or on high for 4-5 hours.
8. With 2 forks, shred the pork while it is still in the slow cooker.
9. Serve the shredded pork with the juices and berries spooned over the top.

Maple Peach Pork Chops

CHOPS

- 4-6 bone-in pork chops
- Sea salt to taste
- Freshly ground black pepper to taste
- 2 TBSP coconut oil

SAUCE INGREDIENTS

- 1 cup chicken broth
- ½ cup pure maple syrup
- 2 TBSP balsamic vinegar
- 1 tsp Dijon mustard
- ¼ cup olive oil
- 1 small shallot, minced

TOPPING

- 3 peaches, peeled, pits removed, and sliced

GARNISH

- 3 TBSP chopped fresh basil

Serves 4

I have a hard time staying away from the slow cooker when these chops are cookin'! The aroma is so, so good—I can't even describe it. Let's just say that if you want the whole neighborhood to smell amazing and you don't mind a few neighbors knocking on your door wanting to be fed, this is the dish to make! You might want to double this recipe in case of unexpected guests.

1. Season the pork chops with sea salt and pepper.
2. In a large skillet, heat the coconut oil over medium-high heat.
3. Place the pork chops in the skillet and brown them on both sides, about 4 minutes total.
4. Transfer the chops to a slow cooker.
5. In a small bowl, combine the sauce ingredients. Pour the sauce over the pork chops, and lay the sliced peaches on top.
6. Cover and cook the chops on low for 5-6 hours or on high for 3-4 hours.
7. Serve the chops with a garnish of chopped basil.

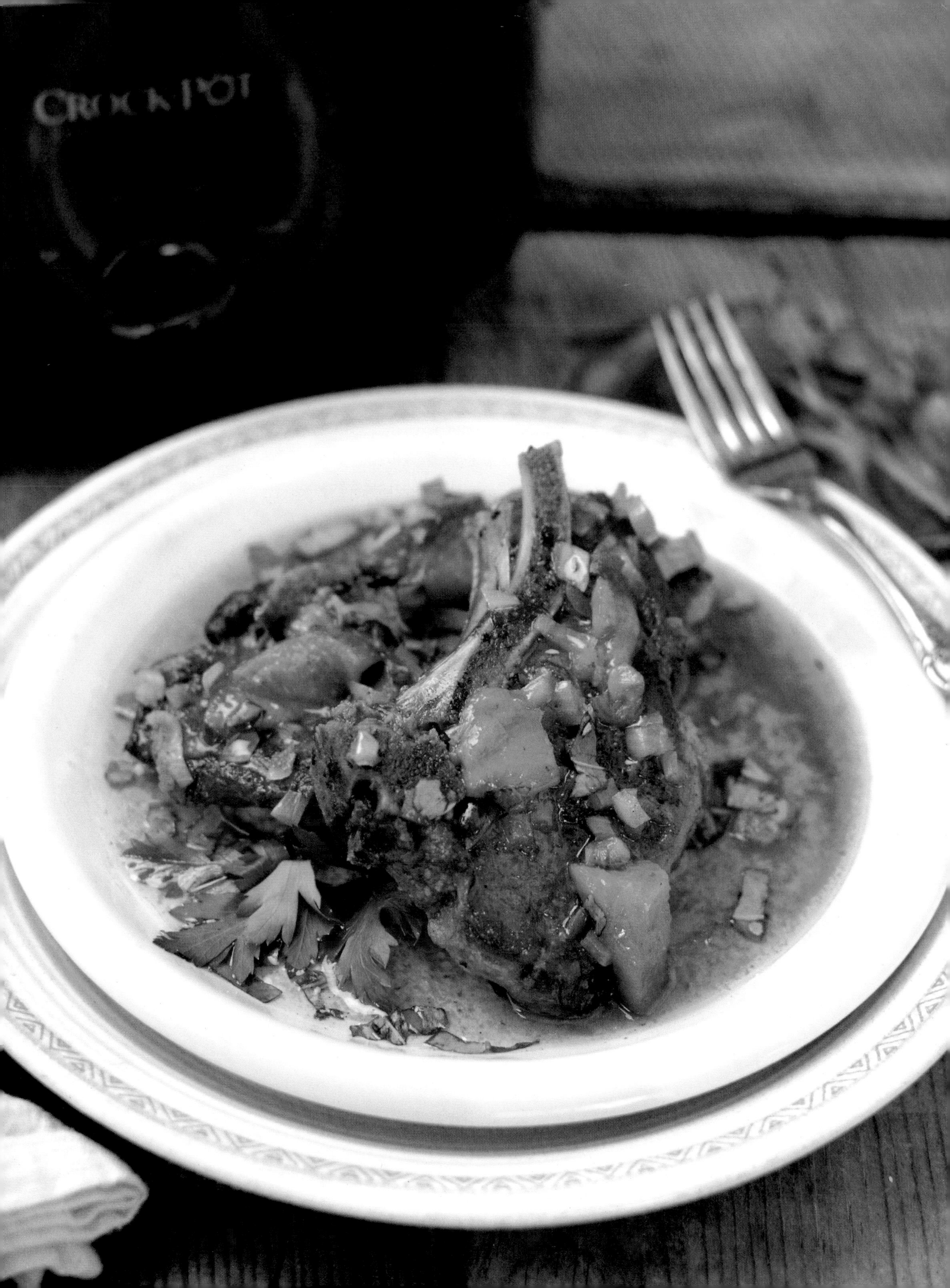
CROCK-POT

Orange Sesame Ginger Pork Roast

ROAST INGREDIENTS

- 4-5-pound pork roast
- 1 tsp sea salt
- Freshly ground black pepper to taste
- 1 tsp dry mustard
- 2 TBSP coconut oil

SAUCE INGREDIENTS

- ½ cup orange juice
- 1 cup beef or chicken broth
- 2 TBSP grated fresh ginger
- 1 TBSP orange zest
- 1 clove garlic, minced
- 1 tsp sesame oil
- 2 TBSP coconut aminos
- 1 TBSP sesame seeds
- 2 TBSP coconut vinegar or apple cider vinegar

Serves 4

I love throwing a handful of ingredients into the slow cooker in the morning, knowing that while I work all day, a tender, juicy, and flavorful dinner is making itself! The flavors of this pork roast are pretty hard to beat, which means that you'll want to buy a really big roast so you'll have leftovers. Coconut vinegar is a fairly new ingredient on store shelves, but if you can find it or order it, I recommend it, because it's fantastic! If not, don't worry; simply substitute raw apple cider vinegar.

1. Sprinkle the roast with the sea salt, pepper, and dry mustard.
2. In a large skillet, melt the coconut oil over medium-high heat.
3. Place the roast in the skillet and brown on all sides, about 8 minutes.
4. Transfer the roast to a slow cooker.
5. In a medium-sized bowl, whisk together the sauce ingredients. Pour the sauce over the roast, and cook it on low for 6-8 hours or on high for 5-6 hours.
6. Serve the roast with the juices spooned over it.

Mushroom Meatballs

MEATBALL INGREDIENTS

- ½ pound ground beef
- ½ pound ground pork
- ½ cup diced yellow onion
- 1 clove garlic, minced
- 1 egg (or 1 TBSP ground flax seeds mixed with 3 TBSP hot water; let it sit for a few minutes until it gels)
- 2 TBSP arrowroot starch
- ¾ tsp sea salt
- ½ tsp freshly ground black pepper
- ¼ tsp allspice
- 2 TBSP coconut oil

SAUCE INGREDIENTS

- 2 cups chicken or beef broth
- 2 cups sliced white button mushrooms
- 1 TBSP Worcestershire sauce
- 1 bay leaf
- 2 cups coconut milk
- 1 TBSP arrowroot starch

GARNISH

- ½ cup chopped fresh parsley

Makes 22 meatballs

This is another nostalgic recipe from my wonderful mom. She used to make a large pan of these mushroom meatballs to fill our tummies with a hearty, satisfying meal. We laugh a little now at the polar-opposite ingredients she used, such as elk burger for the meatballs and canned cream of mushroom soup for the sauce! While the elk was an excellent protein option, the canned, processed, ingredients-that-can't-be-pronounced soup was... not so much. I was so excited to try to upgrade this recipe from canned to fresh, whole ingredients, and the results are pure mushroom perfection!

1. In a medium-sized bowl, combine the beef, pork, onion, garlic, egg, arrowroot starch, sea salt, pepper, and allspice with your hands. Scoop and shape the mixture into 22, 1½-inch meatballs.

2. In a large skillet, heat the coconut oil over medium heat.

3. Add the meatballs to the skillet, leaving space between them so that they brown on all sides.

4. When the meatballs have browned, transfer them to a slow cooker.

5. Add the chicken broth to the skillet and whisk to stir up the yummy browned bits from the bottom.

6. Transfer the broth to the slow cooker.

7. Add the mushrooms, Worcestershire sauce, and bay leaf to the slow cooker and stir gently.

8. Cook the meatballs on low for 4-5 hours or on high for 3-4 hours.

9. In a small bowl, mix the coconut milk and arrowroot starch. Add to the slow cooker during the last 45 minutes of cooking.

10. Serve the meatballs with chopped fresh parsley sprinkled on top.

Bacon & Onion Roast

- 7 slices bacon, chopped
- Sea salt to taste
- Freshly ground black pepper to taste
- 3-4-pound chuck roast
- 2 medium yellow onions, thinly sliced
- ½ cup red wine
- 3 cups beef broth
- 3 cloves garlic, minced

Serves 4

I threw this recipe together one morning with the few ingredients I had on hand. Sometimes the best recipes are created that way! My family devoured the entire roast for dinner and proclaimed it their favorite slow cooker meal ever! Well, you can't get any better than that on a Tuesday night. You can also use brisket for this recipe, but my local butcher doesn't always have one, so I generally opt for a nice fatty chuck roast instead.

1. Cook the bacon in a large skillet over medium-high heat until it is browned and slightly crisp.

2. Remove the bacon with a slotted spoon, and transfer it to a paper towel-lined plate. Set it aside.

3. Sprinkle sea salt and pepper over all sides of the roast. Add the roast to the hot skillet with the bacon grease, and brown it on all sides.

4. Transfer the roast to a slow cooker.

5. Meanwhile, lower the heat under the skillet to medium. Add the onions, and cook, stirring occasionally, until softened, 3-5 minutes.

6. Remove the onions from the skillet, and place them in the slow cooker on and around the roast.

7. Add the wine to the skillet, and scrape any yummy bits of goodness off the bottom of the pan.

8. Add the beef broth and garlic to the skillet, and stir to combine.

9. Pour the wine-broth mixture over the roast, and cook the roast on low for 7-8 hours or on high for 5-6 hours.

10. Serve slices of the roast with the juices, bacon pieces, and onions.

Flank Steak Rellenos

TOMATILLO SALSA INGREDIENTS

- 1 pound tomatillos, papery skins removed
- 2 jalapeños, cored, seeded, and chopped
- 2 cloves garlic, sliced
- ½ small yellow onion, chopped
- ⅓ cup chopped fresh cilantro
- ⅛ tsp cumin
- 1 tsp sea salt
- Freshly ground black pepper to taste

CASHEW CREAM INGREDIENTS

- ¼ cup raw cashews
- 1 clove garlic, sliced
- 2 tsp olive oil
- ½ tsp apple cider vinegar
- Pinch of sea salt
- Freshly ground black pepper to taste
- Some of the cooking liquid
- 1 can (4-ounce) diced green chilies

STEAK INGREDIENTS

- 1½-2 pounds flank steak
- Sea salt to taste
- Freshly ground black pepper to taste
- 2 TBSP coconut oil
- 1 cup chicken or beef broth

Serves 4

1. Wash the tomatillos until they no longer feel sticky. Cut them into quarters and place them in a food processor.

2. Add the remaining salsa ingredients and process until finely chopped.

3. Spoon the salsa into a small saucepan and bring it to a light boil over medium heat.

4. Simmer, stirring occasionally, until most of the liquid has evaporated and the salsa looks slightly thicker, about 10 minutes. Set it aside.

5. For the cashew cream, place the cashews in a small saucepan and cover them with cold water. Bring the liquid to a boil, reduce the heat, and simmer, covered, for 25 minutes.

6. Strain out the cashews, reserving the cooking liquid in a separate bowl.

7. Place the cashews, garlic, olive oil, apple cider vinegar, sea salt, and pepper in the food processor and purée until the mixture begins to become creamy. Slowly add the cooking liquid, 1 TBSP at a time, until the mixture has a thick, creamy consistency.

8. Place the flank steak in a zip-top bag, and pound it with a kitchen mallet to a ½-inch-thickness.

9. Remove the steak from the bag and lay it flat on a clean work surface. Sprinkle it with sea salt and pepper.

10. With a spoon, spread some of the cashew cream down the center of the flank steak. Be careful not to use too much, or it will spread everywhere when you roll it. If your steak is smaller, you may not need to use the entire amount of cashew cream.

11. Sprinkle the diced green chilies over the cashew cream and steak.

12. Roll one of the long edges of the steak over the cream and chilies until you reach the opposite edge. Tie the steak roll in 3 places with butcher's twine.

13. In a large skillet, heat the coconut oil over medium heat. Place the steak roll in the skillet and brown it on all sides.

14. Transfer the steak roll to a slow cooker.

15. Pour the salsa over the steak roll, and add the broth. Cook the steak roll on low for 5-6 hours or on high for 3-4 hours.

16. Remove the twine before slicing the steak roll into pinwheels, and serve with extra sauce.

I'm not gonna lie—this recipe has a few steps to it. But I can tell you that the end result is well worth the extra few minutes of prep! Yet, on some mornings, no matter how much you want to mix a sauce, brown a steak, and while you're at it, prepare a from-scratch six-course meal and wedding cake for your cousin's upcoming nuptials, you just don't have the time. On those days, simply cut your flank steak in half, lay it in the slow cooker, and dump in your favorite green salsa (salsa verde) and a small can of diced green chilies, and you're good to go. Save the extra steps for a day when you have the time and want a little extra something for dinner. Oh, and rellenos traditionally use cream cheese, so if you can tolerate dairy, you can replace the cashew cream with softened cream cheese.

Ginger BBQ Beef

SAUCE INGREDIENTS

- ½ medium yellow onion, diced
- 2 cloves garlic, minced
- 2 tsp minced fresh ginger
- ¼ tsp red pepper flakes
- ½ cup apple juice
- 2 tsp fish sauce
- 1 cup tomato sauce
- 1 can (6-ounce) tomato paste
- 2 TBSP apple cider vinegar
- ½ tsp dry mustard
- Pinch of allspice
- 1 tsp granulated onion
- ½ tsp granulated garlic
- 1 tsp sea salt
- ¼ tsp freshly ground black pepper

BEEF INGREDIENTS

- 4-5 pounds chuck roast
- 2 TBSP coconut oil
- Sea salt to taste
- Freshly ground black pepper to taste

Serves 4

The enticing aroma of this sweet, tangy, and savory roast will call your name by dinnertime! Remember that browning your roast prior to putting it in the slow cooker gives it an appetizing color and deeper flavor, but it isn't a must. If you're having a busy morning, throw all the ingredients in your cooker and turn it to low. By dinner, you'll still have a tender, mouthwatering roast to satisfy that hunger.

1. In a medium-sized bowl, whisk together the sauce ingredients.
2. In a large skillet, heat the coconut oil over medium-high heat.
3. Season the roast with sea salt and pepper and add it to the skillet. Brown the roast on all sides.
4. Transfer the roast to a slow cooker.
5. Pour the sauce over the roast, cover, and cook the roast on low for 6-7 hours or on high for 4-5 hours.
6. When done, shred the roast with 2 forks, and serve with lots of sauce spooned over the top.

Chunky Chili Con Carne

CON CARNE

- 1 pound ground beef
- ½ pound Italian sausage
- ½ pound chuck roast, cubed
- ½ pound boneless pork chops, cubed
- 1 medium yellow onion, diced
- 1 large green bell pepper, chopped
- 2 cloves garlic, minced
- 2 jalapeños, cored, seeded, and diced

SAUCE INGREDIENTS

- 1 can (15-ounce) diced tomatoes
- 1 can (15-ounce) tomato sauce
- 1 can (6-ounce) tomato paste
- 2 cups brewed coffee
- ¼ cup red wine vinegar
- 1 tsp cinnamon
- 3 rounded TBSP chili powder
- 2 rounded tsp cumin
- 2 tsp granulated onion
- 2 tsp granulated garlic
- 1½ tsp sea salt
- ¾ tsp freshly ground black pepper

Serves 4-6

I like to make this huge batch of chili in my big-boy 6-quart slow cooker because I'm sure to have leftovers for lunch the next day. If you don't want to go quite this big, you can use your smaller cooker, but cut the recipe in half. Filled with chunks of beef and pork, this chili satisfies like no other, without a bean in sight!

1. Crumble the ground beef and Italian sausage into a 6-quart slow cooker. Add the chuck roast and pork cubes on top.

2. Sprinkle the onion, bell pepper, garlic, and jalapeños over the meat.

3. In a large bowl, combine the sauce ingredients.

4. Pour the sauce over the meat in the slow cooker.

5. Cook the chili on low for 6-7 hours or on high for 4-5 hours, stirring occasionally.

Roasted Tomato Bacon Soup

- 12 cups fresh tomatoes (about 14 large), on the vine or romas, chopped
- Olive oil for drizzling
- Sea salt to taste
- 10 slices bacon, chopped
- 2 medium yellow onions, chopped
- 2 cups chopped carrots
- 2 cups chopped celery
- 5 cloves garlic, minced
- 2 cups chicken or beef broth
- 1 bay leaf
- 1 cup coconut milk (optional)

Serves 4

If you're looking for something to do with those farmer's market tomatoes that you couldn't resist (I understand—they're beautiful!), try this delicious, smoky tomato soup. I like to prep the ingredients on the stovetop and in the oven. Then I let the slow cooker finish it off so that it's ready for dinner. In a hurry? You can add everything back to the stock pot instead of a slow cooker to finish the cooking (simmer for 30-40 minutes). Just blend it all up when it's hot and the veggies are soft. This soup freezes well, so feel free to make extra, cool it in mason jars, and stick it in the freezer. Reheat this winter to help ward off the winter chill.

1. Preheat your oven to 450°F.
2. Line a baking sheet with foil or parchment paper.
3. Wash and dry the tomatoes. Cut out the stem ends. Slice the tomatoes in half, and place them, cut-side up, on the baking sheet.
4. Drizzle the tomatoes with olive oil, and sprinkle them with sea salt.
5. Place the baking sheet in the oven, and roast the tomatoes for 30 minutes.
6. Remove the tomatoes from the oven, and set them aside.
7. In a large pot or Dutch oven, cook the bacon over medium heat until it is browned and crispy. Remove the bacon with a slotted spoon, and transfer it to a paper towel-lined plate.
8. To the pot with the bacon grease, add the onions, carrots, and celery. Cook, stirring occasionally, until the veggies are soft, about 8-10 minutes.
9. Add the garlic to the pot, and stir.
10. To a slow cooker, add the roasted tomatoes, cooked veggies, broth, bay leaf, and most of the cooked bacon, reserving some for garnish. Cook the soup on low for 4-6 hours.
11. When the soup is done, remove and discard the bay leaf.
12. Purée the soup with an immersion blender. If desired, stir in the coconut milk for a creamy soup, or leave it as is for a traditional consistency.
13. Serve the soup in bowls topped with the extra bacon crumbles.

Veggie Soup

- 5 large tomatoes on the vine
- Olive oil for drizzling
- Sea salt to taste
- 1 cup chopped carrots
- ½ cup chopped celery
- 1 medium yellow onion, chopped
- 5 cloves garlic, minced
- 1 cup chopped white button mushrooms
- 3 cups chicken or beef broth
- 2 TBSP chopped fresh basil
- 2 TBSP chopped fresh parsley
- 1 bay leaf
- 1 tsp sea salt
- ½ tsp freshly ground black pepper
- 1 cup chopped zucchini
- 1 cup chopped spinach or kale

Serves 4

This vibrant, nutrient-dense soup is like a classic minestrone, minus the beans and pasta. Chock full of fresh tomatoes, zucchini, mushrooms, and many other veggies, it's like a bowlful of summer on a cold winter's day. Make an extra-large batch while the ingredients are in season during the summer months, and freeze it in mason jars. You'll get that fresh flavor and nutritional boost that we all miss during those long, gray winter days. If you do plan to freeze it, I recommend using chopped kale instead of spinach. It holds its color and texture better than fragile spinach after freezing and reheating. Oh, and to maximize morning time, chop all your veggies while the tomatoes are in the oven roasting. Everything will go into the slow cooker around the same time, and you'll be out the door in no time!

1. Preheat your oven to 450°F.
2. Line a baking sheet with foil or parchment paper.
3. Wash and dry the tomatoes, and remove the stems. Slice the tomatoes in half, then in half again, making 4 wedges.
4. Place the tomatoes on the baking sheet, drizzle them with olive oil, and sprinkle them with sea salt.
5. Roast the tomatoes in the oven for 20 minutes.
6. Transfer the cooked tomatoes to a slow cooker.
7. Add the carrots, celery, onion, garlic, mushrooms, broth, basil, parsley, bay leaf, sea salt, and pepper to the slow cooker. Cook on low for 4-6 hours.
8. During the last 45 minutes of cooking, add the zucchini and spinach or kale.
9. When the soup is done, remove and discard the bay leaf.
10. Stir the soup to break up the tomatoes, or, if needed, use kitchen scissors to cut the tomatoes into smaller chunks.
11. Enjoy a big bowl of soup or serve alongside your favorite protein.

On the Go

{ portable fare that doesn't disintegrate in your cooler! }

Cocoa Cinnamon Almonds

- 1 tsp cinnamon
- ¼ tsp arrowroot starch
- 2 tsp + 1 tsp cocoa powder
- ½ tsp sea salt
- 2 TBSP pure maple syrup
- 2 cups raw almonds

Makes 2 cups

Who needs plain ol' almonds when you can jazz 'em up with cinnamon and chocolate? This quick snack is great after school, on the road, or packaged in a pretty jar with ribbon as a gift. Delicious and portable!

1. In a small bowl, mix together the cinnamon, arrowroot starch, 2 tsp cocoa powder, and sea salt. Set the mixture aside.

2. Measure the maple syrup into a medium-sized bowl, and set it aside.

3. In a large skillet, toast the almonds over medium-high heat, stirring almost constantly, until the nuts are slightly toasted and hot, 5-8 minutes.

4. Add the almonds to the maple syrup, and toss to coat the nuts.

5. Sprinkle the cocoa powder mixture over the almonds, and stir to coat the nuts evenly.

6. Spread the almonds in a single layer on a parchment-lined baking sheet. Let them cool completely.

7. Once cooled, place the almonds in a zip-top bag. Sprinkle 1 tsp cocoa powder over the almonds, seal the bag, and shake it gently to coat the nuts.

8. Store the almonds in an airtight container, or freeze them until ready to use.

Ginger Orange Pecans

- ¼ tsp sea salt
- ½ tsp ground ginger
- ¼ tsp arrowroot starch
- 2 TBSP pure maple syrup
- 2 cups raw pecans
- 2 tsp orange zest

makes 2 cups

These crunchy, salty, and sweet pecans are like a mouthful of sunshine! The bite of ginger and the freshness of the orange really brighten up the dreariest road trips. Remember to take along a few napkins for this one, as they can be a little sticky (but not too bad). Any fingerprints left in your car will be well worth the trouble, I promise!

1. In a small bowl, mix together the sea salt, ginger, and arrowroot starch. Set the mixture aside.

2. Measure the maple syrup into a medium-sized bowl, and set it aside.

3. In a large skillet, toast the pecans over medium-high heat, stirring almost constantly, until the nuts are slightly toasted and hot, about 5 minutes.

4. Add the pecans to the maple syrup, and toss to coat the nuts.

5. Sprinkle the spice mixture and orange zest over the pecans, and stir to coat them evenly.

6. Spread the pecans in a single layer on a parchment-lined baking sheet. Let them cool completely.

7. Store the pecans in an airtight container, or freeze them until ready to use.

Paleo Party Mix

- 1/3 cup coconut oil, beef tallow, duck fat, or ghee (or a combination)
- 2 TBSP Worcestershire sauce
- 1 tsp gluten-free seasoned salt
- ¼ tsp granulated garlic
- ¼ tsp granulated onion
- 1 cup raw almonds
- 1 cup raw pecans
- 1 cup raw cashews
- ½ cup raw pumpkin seeds
- ½ cup raw sunflower seeds

Makes 4 cups

Oh, how I used to love the flavor and crunch of Chex party mix! I remember munching on it during family Christmas parties where the bottoms of pants were big, and hair and eyeglasses were even bigger. Yeah, well, thank goodness we've outgrown all that! Especially the grains, sugar, and BHT found in that popular cereal. Nowadays, my hair is a lot flatter, and I use nuts and seeds for that yummy crunch. I think butter or ghee makes the flavor here, but you can use any combo of fats you like, such as beef tallow, coconut oil, or duck fat. Try one of the almonds before placing it in the oven to see if it's salty enough for your taste. If not, adjust. I like to add chopped cooked bacon at the end for an even better combo. And if you don't want to use Worcestershire sauce, you can use coconut aminos instead, but cut the salt in half.

1. Preheat your oven to 275°F.
2. Line a baking sheet with parchment paper, and set it aside.
3. In a medium-sized saucepan, melt the coconut oil, fat, or ghee over medium-low heat.
4. Stir in the Worcestershire sauce, seasoned salt, granulated garlic, and granulated onion.
5. Add the almonds, pecans, cashews, pumpkin seeds, and sunflower seeds to the saucepan. Mix well until all the nuts are coated.
6. Spoon the nut mixture onto the lined baking sheet and spread in an even layer.
7. Bake for 45-60 minutes, stirring every 10-15 minutes, until the nuts are nice and toasted.
8. Place the baking sheet on a wire rack to let the nuts cool completely. Store the cooled nuts in a sealed container for 7-10 days.

Nut-Free Granola Bars

- ¼ cup coconut oil
- ¼ cup pure maple syrup
- 2 TBSP coconut nectar
- ¼ cup sunbutter (no sugar added, creamy)
- 1 tsp pure vanilla extract
- ⅓ cup raw pumpkin seeds
- ½ cup roasted salted sunflower seeds
- ⅓ cup raw sunflower seeds
- 1 TBSP sesame seeds
- ¼ cup mini chocolate chips
- ⅓ cup raisins
- ½ cup coconut flakes

Makes 10 bars

Seeds are a great alternative to nuts, but they can get a little boring, according to my eight-year-old. She alternates between pumpkin and sunflower seeds, but she needs them jazzed up occasionally. The maple syrup and sunbutter in these heavenly bars give them an old-fashioned granola bar flavor with all the goodness of natural, real food ingredients and none of the preservatives. Omit the coconut if you can't tolerate it; the recipe is still wonderful!

1. Preheat your oven to 350°F.

2. Line an 8" x 8" square pan with parchment paper, and grease it with coconut oil.

3. In a small saucepan over low heat, combine the coconut oil, maple syrup, coconut nectar, sunbutter, and vanilla extract. Stir occasionally just until the ingredients have melted and mixed. Set the mixture aside to cool, about 15 minutes.

4. In a medium-sized bowl, combine the pumpkin seeds, sunflower seeds (both roasted and raw), sesame seeds, chocolate chips, raisins, and coconut flakes.

5. Pour this coating mixture over the bar mixture in the saucepan. Stir to combine all the ingredients.

6. Spoon the bar mixture into the prepared 8" x 8" pan. Place a sheet of wax paper over the top, and press down firmly with your hands to compress and even out the top of the bars. Remove the wax paper.

7. Bake the bars for 30-35 minutes until bubbly and golden.

8. Remove from the oven and let cool for 1 hour. Cut into bars.

9. Let cool completely. Place the bars in an airtight container and refrigerate them to fully firm them up.

10. Store in the refrigerator for up to a week.

Cracked Pepper
and Chive Crackers

CRACKERS

- ½ cup almond flour
- ¼ cup coconut flour, sifted
- ½ tsp granulated onion
- ¼ tsp sea salt
- ¼ tsp coarsely ground black pepper
- 1 egg
- 1 TBSP coconut oil, melted
- 3 TBSP chopped fresh chives

TOPS

- ¼ tsp coarsely ground black pepper

Makes 30 crackers

On road trips, we like to snack on crackers, salami, olives, etc. So I like to whip up some of these crunchy treats. We love the toasty onion flavor and the little bit of heat from the black pepper. These crispy crackers are perfect with guacamole too!

1. Preheat your oven to 350°F.

2. In a medium-sized bowl, whisk together the almond flour, coconut flour, granulated onion, sea salt, and pepper.

3. Add the egg, and mix well with a hand mixer.

4. Add the coconut oil and chives. Blend again until well incorporated. The dough will be crumbly but should stick together when squeezed in your hand.

5. Roll the dough between 2 sheets of parchment paper. You will have to reshape the edges at times with your hands as it cracks. Roll into a small square, and remove the top piece of parchment.

6. Sprinkle the tops with additional pepper, and press the pepper into the dough with your hands.

7. Using a sharp knife, cut the dough into bite-sized pieces, and place them, while still on the parchment paper, on a baking sheet.

8. Bake the crackers for 9 minutes.

9. Remove the tray from the oven, and carefully pull the crackers apart with a spatula so that they bake more evenly. Bake for another 3-5 minutes or until the centers are cooked and the edges are golden.

10. Let cool on wire racks, and store in an airtight container.

Cashew Lime Hummus

- 1 cup roasted, salted cashews
- ¼ cup coconut milk
- 2 TBSP lime juice
- 1 TBSP coconut aminos
- 2 tsp minced shallot
- Pinch of sea salt
- Freshly ground black pepper to taste

Makes 1 ½ cups

I used to be a recipe addict. I would tear countless recipes from magazines and hold on to them for years in the hope that one day I'd make a delicious item that would become a family favorite forever. Alas, I've grown up a bit since then, and I hate clutter. So I don't tear out recipes anymore. However, I always encourage folks to adapt recipes (even mine) to fit their own needs and tastes. Just because the flavors work for my family doesn't mean that they're perfect for yours, so play! That said, I was cleaning out an old desk drawer and ran across a dip recipe that contained lime and coconut milk. Those two were all I could salvage from the unhealthy ingredients list, but I was inspired to come up with this little creation that my kids love for dipping veggies.

1. Place all the ingredients in a food processor, and purée until smooth. For a thinner dip, add a few additional tablespoons of coconut milk, one at a time, while blending to get the consistency you like.

2. Store the hummus in an airtight container in the refrigerator until ready to use.

3. Dip your favorite veggies, such as carrot sticks, celery sticks, or jicama spears.

Sweet 'n' Smoky Deviled Eggs

EGGS
- 6 eggs, boiled, peeled, and cooled

FILLING INGREDIENTS
- ¼ cup julienne-cut sundried tomatoes
- ⅛ tsp cumin
- 3 strips bacon, chopped, cooked, but not too crispy (reserve some for garnish)
- ¾ tsp smoked paprika
- Sea salt to taste
- Freshly ground black pepper to taste
- ⅓ cup mashed ripe avocado
- 2 TBSP olive oil

GARNISH
- Chopped chives
- Smoked paprika

 Makes 12 eggs

If you're tired of the same ol' deviled eggs, this recipe will get you "egg-cited!" And best of all, you can customize the filling "egg-zactly" how you like. Prefer the flavor of mayo over avocado? You can use Paleo mayo instead, or a little bit of both. Like your filling super creamy? Add as much avocado or mayo as you want! I even like these "chick-a-dees" with a splash of my favorite hot sauce in the filling. Your creativity is your only limit, and that's no "yolk!" Okay, I'm done now.

1. Slice the eggs in half lengthwise. Gently remove the yolks, and place them in a food processor.

2. Set the egg whites aside on a plate.

3. Add the sundried tomatoes, cumin, bacon, paprika, sea salt, pepper, avocado, and olive oil to the food processor (reserve about 2 TBSP of the bacon crumbles for garnish). Pulse until fully combined and smooth. If you like an even creamier filling, you can add additional avocado or mayo until it reaches the desired consistency.

4. With a spoon or piping bag with a decorative tip, fill the egg whites evenly.

5. Sprinkle the eggs with chives, bacon crumbles, and a light sprinkle of smoked paprika.

6. Keep the deviled eggs refrigerated or in a cooler until ready to eat.

Deviled Ham 'n' Eggs

EGGS

- 6 eggs, boiled, peeled, and cooled

FILLING INGREDIENTS

- 2-3 TBSP mayonnaise
- 1 tsp Dijon mustard
- ½ tsp lemon juice
- ½ tsp chopped fresh thyme
- 1 tsp chopped fresh parsley
- ¼ tsp granulated onion
- ¼ tsp granulated garlic
- ½ tsp pure maple syrup
- ¼ tsp sea salt
- Freshly ground black pepper to taste
- ⅓ cup finely diced cooked ham

GARNISH

- 1 tsp chopped fresh thyme

Makes 12 eggs

I find it hard to believe now, but as a kid, I didn't like deviled eggs. I would scoop out the filling and eat just the whites. There was something seriously wrong with me back then; I'm sure of it. Nowadays, I can't get enough of these one-bite flavor explosions! I constantly look for ways to enhance and vary the flavors without taking away from the original, deviled egg essence. I ran across the title of this recipe in a flyer at a local grocery store. I liked the idea of adding ham, so I ran with it. The small addition of fresh thyme and parsley, combined with the smoky ham, is over-the-top fantastic!

1. Cut the eggs in half lengthwise. Remove the yolks, and place them in a small bowl. Set the whites aside on a plate.

2. Mash the yolks with a fork.

3. Add the mayo, mustard, lemon juice, thyme, parsley, granulated onion, granulated garlic, maple syrup, sea salt, and pepper to the mashed yolks, and stir to combine until creamy and smooth. If it's too dry, add additional mayo as needed.

4. Stir the ham into the egg mixture.

5. Fill each egg white half with the ham filling.

6. Top each deviled egg with chopped fresh thyme.

7. Store the deviled eggs in an airtight container in the refrigerator or a cooler until ready to eat.

Creamy Cilantro No Potato Salad

- 1 head cauliflower, cut into large florets
- 4 eggs, boiled, peeled, and chopped
- ½ cup diced dill pickle, or ⅓ cup dill pickle relish
- 3 stalks celery, diced
- 1 cup sliced black olives
- ½ cup chopped fresh cilantro
- ¼ cup diced red onion
- 1 clove garlic, minced
- ½ cup mayonnaise
- 2 tsp Dijon mustard
- 1 TBSP lime juice
- ½ tsp sea salt
- Freshly ground black pepper to taste

Serves a crowd!

First, a big thank you goes to Sarah Fragoso at Everyday Paleo for coming up with the original No Potato Salad made with cauliflower. Genius! Second, this recipe is another example of how I often mess up in the kitchen. One of the best parts of a good potato salad, for me, is the flavor of black olives throughout. And this one's no exception. But wait! Do you see any black olives in the photo? No? That's because I forgot to add them to the bowl before taking a photo of the final dish! Yep, it happens all the time. So take my word for it, because I added the olives post-photo session, and the salad was fantastic. And third, while I don't usually make my own mayo because I don't use it often, I will make a batch for this recipe. The flavor of fresh homemade mayo is well worth the extra prep time.

1. Steam the cauliflower florets for 5-7 minutes. They should be tender but not too soft.

2. Transfer the steamed florets to a medium-sized bowl, and refrigerate them until cool enough to handle, about 15 minutes.

3. Meanwhile, in a large bowl, combine the eggs, pickle, celery, olives, cilantro, onion, garlic, mayo, mustard, lime juice, sea salt, and pepper.

4. Remove the cooled cauliflower from the refrigerator, and chop it into bite-sized pieces. Add it to the rest of salad ingredients. Stir gently to combine.

5. Taste the salad, and add more salt and pepper if needed.

6. Store the salad in an airtight container in the refrigerator or a cooler until needed.

Tip:
Add grilled shrimp, cooked bay shrimp, or diced chicken to the bowl, and make it a meal for the road!

Jicama Carrot Slaw with Grilled Steak

STEAK

- 2 pounds ribeye or sirloin steak, grilled to medium, cut into strips

SLAW INGREDIENTS

- 2 cups shredded green cabbage
- 1 cup julienned carrots
- 1 cup julienned jicama

DRESSING INGREDIENTS

- ¼ cup olive oil
- 2 TBSP lime juice
- 1 TBSP apple cider vinegar
- 1 tsp Dijon mustard
- 1 TBSP pure maple syrup
- 2 tsp minced yellow onion
- 1 tsp minced garlic
- 1 TBSP minced fresh parsley
- 1 tsp hot pepper sauce
- ¼ tsp sea salt
- Pinch of freshly ground black pepper

Serves 4

I made this slaw recently to take on a day trip with my family, and they ate it so quickly that I didn't even get a bite! Good thing I packed other goodies, or I would have starved. (Well, we were 30 minutes from home, so I wouldn't have starved. But I was getting really, really hungry, which is almost the same!) From what I hear, the tangy dressing soaks into the steak pieces, and when combined with the crunchy cabbage, carrots, and jicama . . . well, just make extra. Or so I've learned. You've been warned.

Prep Day:

1. Store the steak strips in an airtight container in the refrigerator or a cooler until needed.

2. In a glass bowl with a lid, combine the cabbage, carrots, and jicama. Refrigerate until needed.

3. In a jar with a tight-fitting lid, combine the dressing ingredients. Shake until fully combined. Refrigerate until needed.

Serving Day:

1. Shake the dressing ingredients to re-combine.

2. Place the steak strips in the bowl with the veggies.

3. Pour the dressing over the slaw and meat, and stir to combine. Enjoy it quickly before it's all gone!

Steak & Chard Salad with Roasted Beets

SALAD INGREDIENTS

- 3 cups chopped chard leaves, thick stems removed
- 1½ pounds ribeye or sirloin steak
- Sea salt to taste
- Freshly ground black pepper to taste
- 2 large beets, peeled and sliced
- Olive oil for drizzling

DRESSING INGREDIENTS

- ½ cup olive oil
- ¼ cup white wine vinegar
- 1 shallot, minced
- 1 clove garlic, minced
- 1 tsp Dijon mustard
- 1 tsp Italian seasoning
- ½ tsp dill
- 1 tsp granulated onion
- ½ tsp sea salt
- Freshly ground black pepper to taste
- 1 tsp honey

Serves 4

For meals on the go, it doesn't get any healthier or easier than this beautiful salad. Make everything a day ahead, and throw it together during your pit stop for a filling and nutritious lunch-a-go-go. Even my kiddos, who think they don't like chard, annihilate this salad because it's a salad, not chard. And who am I to argue with this logic?

1. Preheat your oven to 450°F, and heat your grill to medium-high heat.

2. Place the chard in an airtight container, and place it in the refrigerator or a cooler.

3. Season the steak with sea salt and pepper. Grill the steak to medium, about 4 minutes per side, depending on its thickness. Set it aside to cool.

4. Line a baking sheet with parchment paper. Place the beet slices in a single layer on the baking sheet. Drizzle the beets with olive oil, and sprinkle them with sea salt and pepper.

5. Roast the beets in the oven for 15-20 minutes or until soft. Then set them aside to cool.

6. In a jar with a tight-fitting lid, combine the dressing ingredients. Shake to mix well. Store in the refrigerator or a cooler.

7. Slice the steak into strips, place them in an airtight container, and store in the refrigerator or a cooler.

8. Cut the beet slices in half, place them in an airtight container, and store them in the refrigerator or a cooler.

9. When you're ready to eat your salad, simply place the chopped chard in a bowl, and top it with the steak strips and beets. Drizzle on the dressing, and you're all set!

Tomato Avocado Salad with Grilled Chicken

SALAD INGREDIENTS

- 2½ cups cubed grilled chicken
- 2 large heirloom tomatoes (or beefsteak)
- 2 small avocados
- 4 or 5 basil leaves, torn into smaller pieces
- 1 cup black olives, sliced in half
- ¼ cup diced red onion

DRESSING INGREDIENTS

- ¼ cup olive oil
- 1 TBSP lemon juice
- 1 TBSP balsamic vinegar
- 1 tsp Dijon mustard
- 2 tsp coconut aminos
- ½ tsp oregano
- ¼ tsp tarragon
- ½ tsp basil
- ⅛ tsp sea salt
- Pinch of freshly ground black pepper

Serves 4

There is nothing better than summer-ripe tomatoes with a light vinaigrette to bring out their intense flavors! You can use your favorite tomatoes here, but I highly recommend splurging on some organic heirlooms. The colors and textures they bring to this salad can't be beat. While my whole family enjoys this particular combo, you can vary the ingredients and change it up however you like. This salad would be great with steak instead of chicken and perhaps some mushrooms or bell peppers. Use the recipe as a jumping-off point to let your imagination fly!

1. Place the chicken in a large bowl with a lid.

2. Cut the tomatoes in half, and then into thin wedges. Add them to the bowl with the chicken.

3. Cut the avocados in half, and remove the pits. Slice the flesh lengthwise. Using a spoon, gently scoop out each avocado half. Separate the slices, and place them in the bowl with the tomatoes and chicken.

4. Add the basil, olives, and onion to the bowl.

5. In a jar with a tight-fitting lid, combine the dressing ingredients. Shake well, and pour the dressing over the salad. Use as much or as little as you'd like.

6. Cover and refrigerate the salad until needed.

7. Stir the salad before serving.

Citrus Red Onion Slaw with Grilled Chicken

SALAD INGREDIENTS

- 1 medium head green cabbage, thinly sliced
- 1 small red onion, thinly sliced
- 2 TBSP chopped fresh cilantro
- ½ cup chopped celery
- 2 cups cubed cooked chicken (I like to grill mine)
- Sea salt to taste
- Freshly ground black pepper to taste
- ½ cup toasted walnuts

DRESSING INGREDIENTS

- ½ cup orange juice
- 2 TBSP lemon juice
- 2 TBSP apple cider vinegar
- ¼ cup olive oil
- 1 tsp Dijon mustard
- 2 tsp honey
- 1 clove garlic, minced
- ½ tsp sea salt
- Freshly ground black pepper to taste

Serves 4

Want to know a secret? I originally created this recipe with red cabbage. I had it all planned out, with the recipe jotted down. Then I went to prepare it one sunny afternoon, and bam! No red cabbage in the house. How did that happen? I was writing a book, for heaven's sake. I shouldn't make those mistakes! But I do. All. The. Time. Why am I telling you about my incompetence? Well, because I want folks to understand that no one is perfect, and sometimes you just have to roll with the punches, be flexible, and think outside the recipe box. I had green cabbage on hand, knew it would taste great, and changed the name accordingly. Voilà! Citrus Red Onion Slaw! Don't let small hurdles get in your way in the kitchen. Think of a fun way to come up with something new. Oh, and if you'd rather use red cabbage, feel free. It works!

1. In a large bowl, combine the salad ingredients.

2. In a jar with a tight-fitting lid, combine the dressing ingredients. Shake well, and pour it over the salad. Toss to coat.

3. Store the salad in the refrigerator or a cooler until ready to eat.

Grilled Chicken Antipasto Salad

SALAD INGREDIENTS

- 1½ cups pitted kalamata olives
- 2 cups artichoke hearts, frozen or in water (be sure to squeeze out any excess water with a paper towel)
- 1 cup julienne-cut sundried tomatoes
- 8 ounces salami, sliced into wedges
- 1½ cups diced grilled chicken
- 3 TBSP chopped fresh basil (about 8 leaves)
- 3 TBSP chopped fresh parsley

DRESSING INGREDIENTS

- ⅔ cup olive oil
- ⅓ cup white wine
- 2 TBSP minced shallot
- 1 clove garlic, minced
- 1½ tsp Dijon mustard
- 1¼ tsp Italian seasoning
- 1 tsp granulated garlic
- 1 tsp honey
- ½ tsp sea salt
- Freshly ground black pepper to taste

Serves 4-6

My original antipasto salad recipe appeared in *Paleo Indulgences* and has been a family favorite for years. While we have enjoyed that particular version many times, I realized recently that it is more of a delicious side dish than a main meal when taken on the road. So I added grilled chicken, swapped the black olives for kalamatas, updated the dressing, and increased the measurements to feed a crowd. Now I have a one-bowl meal that travels well, and the whole family can enjoy it! Every once in a while, just to keep things interesting, I add chopped cooked bacon, pickled asparagus, mushrooms, or chopped raw cauliflower. This one's best made the day before so that it soaks up the dressing and gets all yummified!

1. In a large bowl, combine the salad ingredients. Set aside.
2. In a jar with a tight-fitting lid, combine the dressing ingredients. Shake to mix well.
3. Pour the dressing over the salad, and toss to coat.
4. Cover the salad, and refrigerate it until needed.
5. Stir the salad again before serving.

Tomato Salad with Jalapeño Vinaigrette

SALAD INGREDIENTS

- 2 pints (32 ounces) cherry tomatoes, sliced in half
- 2 TBSP finely diced red onions
- 2 TBSP chopped cilantro

DRESSING INGREDIENTS

- 1 clove garlic, minced
- 1 TBSP minced shallot
- 1 small jalapeño, cored, seeded, and diced
- 1 TBSP lime juice
- 1 TBSP apple cider vinegar
- ¼ cup olive oil
- 1 TBSP honey
- ¼ tsp chipotle chili powder
- Pinch of sea salt
- Freshly ground black pepper to taste

Serves 4

I love the versatility of a cherry tomato salad. By simply swapping the dressing with another favorite, you can create an entirely new dish with very little effort. And I'm all for very little effort in the kitchen! Try this one with the dressing from the Grilled Chicken Antipasto Salad on page 168 for a satisfying change of pace.

1. In a medium-sized bowl, combine the salad ingredients.
2. In a food processor or bullet blender, combine the dressing ingredients. Process until all the ingredients are well blended, although some small chunks are fine.
3. Pour the dressing over the salad, and toss to coat.
4. Refrigerate the salad, or place it in a cooler until ready to eat.
5. Stir the salad again before serving.

Chicken & Egg Salad Stuffed Peppers

SALAD

- 2 cups diced cooked chicken
- 2 hardboiled eggs, peeled and chopped
- 1 stalk celery, chopped
- 1 green onion, chopped
- 1 TBSP chopped fresh parsley
- ½ tsp dill
- ½ tsp Dijon mustard
- 2 TBSP mayonnaise
- ⅛ tsp granulated onion
- Sea salt to taste
- Freshly ground black pepper to taste
- Squeeze of lemon juice

SPOONS

- 2 carrots, peeled

PEPPERS

- 4 bell peppers, any color you'd like

GARNISH

- Chopped toasted almonds

Makes 4 peppers

Which came first—the chicken or the egg? I say, who cares! Let's throw them both together and make something delicious. Whether on the road in a cooler or in a lunchbox for school, this healthy meal fills them up and keeps 'em going. My kids adore this lunch on-the-go, especially the carrot spoons. I take an extra minute to scrape out a carrot stick so that they can use it as a spoon. That way, they can eat every bit of it, spoon and all! Hey, if it gets them to eat some extra veggies because it's fun, it's worth the extra time.

1. In a medium-sized bowl, stir together the salad ingredients until well blended. Set aside.

2. Cut the ends off of the carrots. Cut off the skinny end, leaving a 4-inch piece on the fatter end. Cut this piece in half. Using a teaspoon, scrape out a well in the fattest part of the carrot to create a spoon. Do so for all 4 pieces.

3. Cut the stem tops off of the bell peppers. With a spoon, scrape out the white ribs and seeds.

4. Fill each pepper with the chicken and egg salad.

5. Store the dish in an airtight container in the refrigerator or a cooler until ready to eat.

6. Top each pepper with toasted almonds, and serve with a carrot spoon.

BLAST Sushi (bacon, lettuce, avocado & sundried tomatoes)

PER SUSHI ROLL/LOG

- 2 slices bacon
- 4 slices avocado
- 1 large romaine lettuce leaf
- 1-2 TBSP julienne-cut sundried tomatoes
- 1 sheet nori

PLUS

- Bamboo rolling mat to properly roll your sushi
- Chopped black olives for garnish

Make what you need

We love making sushi at home, but I'm always a little concerned about taking it in a cooler, in case the temperature fluctuates more than that delicate crab meat will allow. I don't know about you, but food poisoning on a road trip is something I try hard to avoid! So I came up with this little twist on the BLT to keep everything contained in a nice little wrap and still get my sushi-ish fix while on the road.

1. Cook the bacon until done but not too crisp. Let cool.
2. When the bacon is cool, slice it lengthwise into thin strips.
3. Slice the romaine leaf in half, remove the center rib, and discard it.
4. On the edge (closest to you) of the nori, place a half leaf of lettuce, a slice of bacon, a slice of avocado, some tomatoes, and the other half leaf of lettuce on top to cushion the bacon from poking through the nori. Roll tightly.
5. Slice the roll with a very sharp knife and place in an airtight container. Refrigerate until needed.
6. To enjoy, dip the sushi pieces in Paleo Ranch Dressing (recipe follows) and sprinkle a few chopped black olives on top.

Paleo Ranch Dressing

- 1 cup mayonnaise
- ¼-1/3 cup coconut milk (less for a thicker dressing, more for a thinner dressing)
- Pinch of sea salt
- Freshly ground black pepper to taste
- ½ tsp finely minced garlic (about half a clove)
- 2 TBSP chopped fresh dill
- 3 TBSP chopped fresh parsley
- 1 TBSP chopped fresh chives

Makes 1 1/4 cups

1. In a small bowl, whisk together all the ingredients. Try to make it the day before for best flavor, but a minimum of 1 hour in advance.
2. To serve, dip the sushi rolls in the ranch dressing, and enjoy the heck out of it!

Thai Chicken Drumsticks

- 3-5 pounds chicken legs, with skin
- ½ cup loosely packed cilantro
- 2 cloves garlic, sliced
- 2 TBSP fish sauce
- ¼ cup lime juice
- ½-inch piece of fresh ginger, sliced
- 1 small shallot, sliced
- 2 TBSP olive oil
- 2 TBSP coconut aminos
- 1 TBSP honey
- 2 TBSP coconut milk

Serves 4

You'd better make extras of these scrumptious drumsticks, because they go fast! Who knew picnic fare could be so flavorful? But they're not just for your next road trip. We like these so much that they've become a staple weeknight meal at home. If you like things on the spicy side, add some red pepper flakes to the sauce for some kick.

1. Preheat your oven to 375°F. Grease a 9" x 13" baking dish. Distribute the chicken legs evenly in the dish.

2. Place the rest of the ingredients in a food processor. Pulse until chopped. You should end up with a thick but slightly chunky sauce.

3. Pour the sauce evenly over the chicken. Bake for 30 minutes.

4. Remove the pan from the oven, flip the chicken, and spoon the sauce from the pan over each leg. Put the pan back in the oven and bake for another 30 minutes, or until chicken is browned and cooked through.

5. Enjoy hot or cool slightly, or place in containers and refrigerate until needed.

Best Ever Chicken Strips

#1 PAN
- ½ cup arrowroot starch
- ½ tsp sea salt
- ½ tsp freshly ground black pepper

#2 BOWL
- 2 eggs

#3 PAN
- ½ cup coconut flour, sifted
- ½ tsp sea salt
- ½ tsp freshly ground black pepper
- ¾ tsp granulated onion
- ½ tsp granulated garlic
- ½ tsp paprika
- ¼ tsp turmeric

CHICKEN
- ¾ cup coconut oil (or tallow, lard, or duck fat)
- 5 boneless, skinless chicken breasts, cut into 1-inch strips

Serves 4

1. Preheat your oven to 300°F.

2. Place a metal cooling rack on a baking sheet, and set aside.

3. In a shallow pan, place the #1 pan ingredients, and stir to combine.

4. In a bowl (#2), whisk the eggs, and set aside.

5. In a shallow pan, place the #3 pan ingredients. Stir to combine, and set aside.

6. In a large skillet, heat the coconut oil over medium heat. You want enough oil to come halfway up the sides of the chicken strips.

7. With a fork, pick up a chicken strip, and place it in the arrowroot mixture (#1 pan). Toss it to coat.

8. Next, put the coated strip in the whisked eggs (#2 bowl), and turn it to coat.

9. Move the strip to the coconut flour mixture (#3 pan), and turn it to coat.

10. Place the strip in the skillet. Repeat steps 7-9 with the additional chicken strips until the pan is full but not crowded. The chicken strips should not touch each other.

11. Cook the chicken on one side until it is browned, about 2 minutes. Then turn the strips, and continue cooking until the other side is nicely browned, about 2 minutes more.

12. Place the browned chicken strips on the metal cooling rack on top of the baking sheet, and place the whole thing in the oven to cook while you fry the remaining strips.

13. Continue to place browned strips on the rack until the last one is done. Leave the pan in the oven for an additional 8 minutes after adding the last strip.

14. Remove the pan from the oven, and let the strips cool to room temperature, but for no longer than 1 hour.

15. Place the chicken strips in an airtight container, separating the rows with wax paper. Refrigerate until needed. Serve with the Honey Mustard and Spicy Avocado dipping sauces (page 180).

Fried chicken is the perfect picnic food, but it can be labor-intensive and, of course, is covered in flour. I wanted something similar in flavor that was portable for road trips. After trying many nut crusts that always fell off prior to eating, I landed on this combination of ingredients that delivers a nice coating that stays put. The trick is the double-dip of arrowroot and then the coconut flour, along with letting the strips cool on wire racks so that they aren't lying on a plate getting soggy on the bottoms. We like a variety of dipping sauces, so I usually bring along my Paleo Ranch Dressing (page 174) and the Honey Mustard and Spicy Avocado (page 180). The only question now is: Where are you going on your next road trip?

Honey Mustard Dipping Sauce

- 2 TBSP Dijon mustard
- 2 TBSP yellow mustard
- 3 TBSP honey
- ½ tsp granulated onion
- ¼ tsp granulated garlic
- ¼ tsp sea salt
- Pinch of freshly ground black pepper

Makes 1/3 cup

1. In a small bowl, stir together all the ingredients. Cover and refrigerate until needed.

Spicy Avocado Dipping Sauce

- 1 large ripe avocado, halved, pit discarded
- 1 jalapeño, cored, seeded, and minced
- 1 TBSP chopped fresh cilantro
- 2 TBSP mayonnaise
- 2 tsp lime juice
- ½ tsp hot sauce

Makes 1 cup

1. Scoop the avocado flesh from the skins, and place it in a small bowl.
2. Add the remaining ingredients and mash with a fork until fairly smooth and fully combined.
3. Cover and refrigerate until needed.

Shrimp Rolls with Nutty Ginger Sauce

ROLL INGREDIENTS

- 8 spring roll skins
- 4 green leaf lettuce leaves
- 16 large cooked shrimp, tails removed
- 1 small bunch cilantro
- 1 carrot, cut into matchsticks

SAUCE INGREDIENTS

- ⅓ cup almond butter
- 2-3 TBSP coconut milk
- ½ tsp minced fresh ginger
- 1 TBSP lime juice
- Pinch of red pepper flakes
- 1 small clove garlic, finely minced
- 1 TBSP coconut aminos
- 1/2 tsp sesame oil
- 1/2 tsp apple cider vinegar

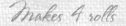

Makes 4 rolls

1. In a shallow pan of lukewarm water, place 2 spring roll skins, and let them soak for 10-15 seconds to soften them slightly. Be careful when handling, as they break easily when brittle.

2. Gently remove the skins from the water, and place them on a kitchen towel. Let them rest for about 30 seconds to become more pliable.

3. Arrange 1 piece of lettuce on the bottom half of 1 skin. You can tear the leaf so it fits nicely. Leave a 1-inch border around the edge of the spring roll skin.

4. Evenly distribute 4 shrimp, a little cilantro, and some carrots over the spring roll skin. Be sure not to overfill, which can cause the skin to break when rolling.

5. Pressing down on the filling with your fingers, fold the left and right sides inward, and then start rolling the end nearest you over the top of the fillings and to the other side. If the skin gets too dry to seal, moisten the unsealed edges with a little warm water.

6. Place the completed roll on a plate, seam side down, and cover with a damp paper towel. Repeat with the remaining ingredients.

7. Shrimp rolls can be made a day ahead. Simply cover them with a damp paper towel, wrap them well in plastic wrap, and place them in an airtight container. Store in the refrigerator or a cooler until ready to use.

8. In a medium-sized bowl, combine the sauce ingredients and whisk until fully combined.

9. Store the sauce in a jar with a tight-fitting lid in the refrigerator until needed.

10. To serve, cut the rolls on a diagonal, and serve them with the sauce.

Coffee Rubbed
Steak Strips

CONTAINER #1

- 1½ tsp finely ground coffee
- ¼ tsp chili powder
- 1 tsp granulated onion
- ½ tsp dry mustard
- ¾ tsp paprika
- ¾ tsp sea salt
- Freshly ground black pepper to taste
- 1½-2 pounds steak, cut into strips (I like top sirloin or New York strip)
- 2 TBSP honey, slightly warmed if needed, for drizzling
- 3 cloves garlic, minced

CONTAINER #2

- 2 TBSP coconut oil

Serves 4

The intoxicating smell and delicious taste of coffee is one of the miracles of this world. So, why limit its use to just that morning jolt? I'm a big fan of using coffee to enhance the chocolate flavor of a dessert or the savory goodness of an amazing steak. My family likes this dish on the sweeter side to offset the bitterness of the coffee, but adjust the amount of honey to suit your taste. And feel free to turn up the heat with additional chipotle powder or cayenne. Go ahead, live it up a little!

Prep Day:

1. In a small bowl, mix the coffee, chili powder, granulated onion, mustard, paprika, sea salt, and pepper.

2. In a 1-gallon zip-top bag, add the steak strips, honey, garlic, and spice mixture. Remove any air from the bag, and seal. Using your hands, squish the meat and spices around to coat all the pieces of meat.

3. Store the bag in the refrigerator or a cooler until ready to use.

Serving Day:

1. In an electric skillet set to medium-high heat, heat the coconut oil.

2. Add the seasoned steak strips to the skillet, stir to coat them in the oil, and let them sit without touching so that they brown slightly, about 2 minutes.

3. Cook, stirring occasionally, until the steak is browned but remains pink inside, about 3 more minutes.

Ribeye Nuggets with Jalapeño Pesto

So, how hot do you like it? I'm talking jalapeños here, so don't let your mind wander! I like a little bit of spice, but not too much. So I remove both the seeds and the ribs from my jalapeños. The seeds contain most of the heat, but it's also in those white ribs. The easiest way to prep your jalapeños is to cut off the stem end and split the pepper in half lengthwise. Using a small spoon, scrape out some (or a lot) of the ribs and seeds. Make sure to wash your hands afterward! The oils from the pepper can linger, which means that the next time you touch your nose or eyes ... ouch!

Prep Day:

1. Place the steak pieces and coconut oil in separate airtight containers (#1 and #2).

2. In a food processor, purée the pesto ingredients until smooth. Add more olive oil if needed to get the consistency you like.

3. Spoon the pesto into airtight container #3.

4. Store the containers in the refrigerator or a cooler until ready to use.

Serving Day:

1. In an electric skillet set to medium-high heat, heat the coconut oil.

2. When the oil is hot, add the steak pieces to the skillet. Season the steak with sea salt and pepper, and cook until it has browned on all sides but is still pink inside, about 5 minutes.

3. Serve the steak with pesto drizzled on top.

Red Curry Steak Fajitas

- 1 TBSP red curry paste
- ¼ cup olive oil
- ¼ cup lime juice
- 1 TBSP honey
- 2 tsp coconut aminos
- 1 small shallot, minced
- 2 cloves garlic, minced
- ½ tsp sea salt
- Freshly ground black pepper to taste

CONTAINER #2

- 2 pounds skirt steak (or your favorite cut), sliced

CONTAINER #3

- 1 red or orange bell pepper, sliced
- ½ yellow onion, sliced

CONTAINER #4

- ¼ cup chopped, fresh cilantro

CONTAINER #5

- 3 TBSP coconut oil

Serves 4

Don't let the name of this dish fool you. Red curry doesn't taste anything like its yellow and green counterparts, so if you tend to shy away from anything called "curry," you might want to give this one a try! Red curry paste can be very spicy depending on the brand, so experiment a little and find one that suits your taste. I use the Thai Kitchen brand, and I don't find it spicy (as in hot), but almost smoky in flavor. Feel free to play with the levels of red curry paste and honey to get just the right balance for you!

Prep Day:

1. In a food processor, blend the sauce ingredients until smooth.
2. Place the sauce in airtight container #1, and refrigerate until needed.
3. Place the steak slices in airtight container #2, and refrigerate until needed.
4. Place the sliced bell pepper and onion in airtight container #3, and refrigerate until needed.
5. Place the cilantro and coconut oil in separate airtight containers (#4 and #5), and refrigerate the cilantro only.

Serving Day:

1. In an electric skillet set to medium heat, heat the coconut oil.
2. Add the bell pepper and onion, and cook, stirring occasionally, until softened, about 3 minutes.
3. Add the steak, and cook, stirring occasionally, until the steak has browned, about 3 minutes.
4. Add the red curry sauce, and stir. Simmer, uncovered, for 1-2 minutes or until the steak is done and the sauce is warm. Serve with a sprinkle of chopped cilantro on top.

Travel Treats

{ sweeter treats that travel well! }

Almond Shortbread

DRY INGREDIENTS

- 1 cup almond flour
- ¼ cup coconut flour, sifted
- ⅔ cup arrowroot starch
- ½ tsp sea salt
- ¼ cup coconut sugar

WET INGREDIENTS

- ¼ cup pure maple syrup
- ½ tsp pure almond extract
- ¼ cup coconut oil, melted

ADD-IN

- ½ cup coarsely chopped raw almonds

Makes 9 cookies

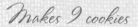

Shortbread is essentially flour and butter. That's it! Yet, it's amazing. Well, I used to think so before going Paleo. Nowadays, I make this version with heart-healthy coconut oil and almond flour, creating an amazingly decadent, melt-in-your-mouth shortbread that rivals the original. If you must have that buttery flavor and can tolerate dairy, you can sub ½ cup of softened butter for the coconut oil. You can also change this one with some chopped pecans or other flavors such as orange zest, cocoa powder, or cinnamon. What's your favorite flavor?

1. Preheat your oven to 350°F.
2. In a small bowl, combine the almond flour, coconut flour, arrowroot starch, and sea salt.
3. In a coffee grinder or food processor, grind the coconut sugar into a powder.
4. In a medium-sized bowl, blend the powdered coconut sugar, maple syrup, and almond extract until combined.
5. Add the contents of the small bowl to the medium-sized bowl, and mix to combine.
6. Slowly add the coconut oil to the mixture, and blend well.
7. Stir in the chopped almonds.
8. Roll the dough between the 2 sheets of parchment paper to ½-inch-thickness.
9. Using a circle cookie cutter, cut out 9 cookie shapes. If needed, remove any excess dough, re-roll it, and cut it out. If the dough is too sticky, dust the parchment paper with some extra arrowroot starch.
10. Peel off the top piece of parchment paper. Place the bottom piece, with the cookies, directly on a baking sheet.
11. Bake for 15-18 minutes or until the cookies are golden brown.
12. Let the shortbread cool completely on a wire rack.
13. Store in an airtight container or freeze until ready to eat.

Chocolate Almond Butter Swirls

DRY INGREDIENTS
- 1 cup almond flour
- 2 TBSP coconut flour, sifted
- ⅓ cup arrowroot starch
- ½ tsp baking soda
- Pinch of sea salt

WET INGREDIENTS
- 2 TBSP pure maple syrup
- 1 egg
- 2 tsp pure vanilla extract
- ¼ cup almond butter
- 2 TBSP coconut sugar (dry crystals)
- 2 TBSP coconut oil, melted

ADD-INS
- ½ cup mini chocolate chips
- 2 TBSP cocoa powder
- 2 tsp water

Makes 12 cookies

When you start eating Paleo, you think that you'll never bake again, let alone make eye-catching treats because the ingredients, and therefore the doughs, are so different from traditional baking. But after playing with ingredients and dry-to-liquid ratios, you find that you can make plenty of beautiful desserts without wheat flour! These cookies are the perfect example, and a great blend of chocolate and almond butter swirled into a big soft cookie. The kids flip for these!

1. Preheat your oven to 350°F.

2. In a small bowl, combine the almond flour, coconut flour, arrowroot starch, baking soda, and sea salt. Set the bowl aside.

3. In a medium-sized bowl, blend the maple syrup, egg, vanilla extract, almond butter, coconut sugar, and coconut oil with a hand mixer until well combined and the coconut sugar has mostly dissolved.

4. Add the contents of the small bowl to the medium-sized bowl, and mix well.

5. Stir in the chocolate chips.

6. Divide the dough in half, and place one half in another bowl.

7. Add the cocoa powder and water to one half of the dough, and mix with your hands to incorporate.

8. Shape 1-inch dough balls of both the plain dough and the chocolate dough. Take 1 ball of each, lightly press them together, and roll them in your palms to make them swirl.

9. Place the cookies on a parchment-lined baking sheet.

10. Bake for 10-12 minutes or until the bottoms are lightly browned. (I take mine out at 10 minutes because I like them a little doughy in the center.)

11. Let the Swirls cool on wire racks.

12. Store the Swirls in an airtight container, or freeze them until ready to eat.

Chocolate Dipped Strawberry Macaroons

COOKIE INGREDIENTS

- 1 bag (1.2 ounces) freeze-dried strawberries
- 5 egg whites
- ⅛ tsp sea salt
- ¼ cup honey
- 2 tsp pure vanilla extract
- 2 cups finely shredded coconut, unsweetened
- 3 TBSP coconut flour, sifted

CHOCOLATE DIP INGREDIENTS

- ¾ cup chopped dark chocolate
- 1 tsp palm shortening

Makes 18 cookies

There's a great company out there called Hail Merry that makes amazingly delicious gluten-free, grain-free, dairy-free, and refined sugar-free treats like macaroons and mini-tarts. And let me tell you, they are wondrous! They've inspired me to create my own versions. I took one bite of their strawberry macaroons and knew that I had to learn to make my own, as I didn't want to leverage the house to buy the quantity I wanted to consume. While Hail Merry's version is hard to beat, my version gets the cravings taken care of in the comfort of my own, unleveraged home.

1. Preheat your oven to 350°F.

2. In a food processor, purée half the bag of freeze-dried strawberries until it becomes a fine powder. Be sure to remove any moisture packet from the bag first! (I may have puréed the packet with the strawberries once. Maybe.)

3. Coarsely chop the other half of the strawberries.

4. In a medium-sized bowl, beat the egg whites with the sea salt with a hand mixer until stiff peaks form.

5. Gently fold the strawberry powder, chopped strawberries, and remaining ingredients into the stiff egg whites just until combined. Don't mix too vigorously, or you'll lose the air in the egg whites.

6. Scoop the dough into golf ball-sized balls, and place them on parchment-lined baking sheets.

7. Bake the cookies for 13-15 minutes or until the bottoms turn golden brown.

8. Place the baking sheet on a wire rack and let the cookies cool completely.

9. Meanwhile, melt the dark chocolate and shortening in the top of a double boiler over simmering water, stirring until smooth.

10. Dip the bottom of each cooled cookie into the melted chocolate. Place the cookies on a wax paper-lined baking sheet until the chocolate hardens.

11. Store the cookies in an airtight container in the refrigerator, or freeze them until needed.

Kitchen Sink Cookies

DRY INGREDIENTS
- 1 cup almond flour
- 3 TBSP coconut flour, sifted
- ¼ cup arrowroot starch
- ¼ cup tapioca starch
- ½ tsp baking soda
- ¼ tsp cinnamon
- Pinch of sea salt

WET INGREDIENTS
- 2 eggs
- 2 tsp pure vanilla extract
- ¼ tsp pure almond extract
- ¼ cup pure maple syrup
- 2 TBSP coconut oil, melted
  (or 3 TBSP softened butter)

ADD-INS
- ¼ cup chocolate chips
- ¼ cup raw pecans, chopped
- ¼ cup unsweetened coconut flakes
- ¼ cup raisins

Makes 12 cookies

Ahh, I love a recipe that has no hard-and-fast rules. As the name implies, you can throw whatever you'd like into these bad boys . . . well, anything but the kitchen sink! My favorite combo is shown here: chocolate chips, pecans, coconut flakes, and raisins. But we use whatever we have on hand. Got dried cherries? Throw 'em in! Some leftover Paleo granola? You betcha! Anything goes with this wonderful cookie base, so get creative!

1. In a medium-sized bowl, stir together the almond flour, coconut flour, arrowroot starch, tapioca starch, baking soda, cinnamon, and sea salt until well combined.

2. Add the eggs, vanilla extract, almond extract, and maple syrup, and blend until just combined.

3. Add the coconut oil, and mix well.

4. Stir in your favorite add-ins.

5. Scoop the dough into 2-inch balls.

6. At this point, you can bake the cookies or freeze the dough for later. To freeze, place the dough balls on a wax paper-lined baking sheet, and place the sheet in the freezer. Once frozen, transfer the dough balls to a freezer-safe zip-top bag, and freeze until needed.

7. When you're ready to bake the cookies, preheat your oven to 350°F.

8. Place the dough balls on a parchment-lined baking sheet. Leave some space between them, as the cookies will spread a little if you have used butter.

9. Bake for 12-13 minutes or until the edges and bottoms are golden brown.

10. Place the baking sheet on a cooling rack, and let the cookies cool completely.

11. Store the cookies in an airtight container, or freeze them until ready to eat.

Orange White Chocolate Macadamia Cookies

DRY INGREDIENTS
- 2 cups almond flour
- 2 TBSP coconut flour, sifted
- ⅓ cup arrowroot starch
- 1 tsp baking soda
- ½ tsp sea salt

WET INGREDIENTS
- ¼ cup pure maple syrup
- 2 tsp pure vanilla extract
- 1 egg (or 2 TBSP applesauce)
- 2 TBSP coconut oil, melted (or 3 TBSP softened butter)

ADD-INS
- Zest of 1 orange
- ½ cup white chocolate chips
- ½ cup coarsely chopped roasted macadamia nuts

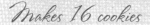
Makes 16 cookies

Long ago during the holidays, I made huge batches of these cookies with wheat flour, sugar, and who knows what else. I gave them up for many years because I just couldn't replicate that same flavor in a gluten-free cookie. Until now! I'm over the moon for these orange-scented sweethearts, and I think you will be, too. As for the white chocolate chips, you have options. Many health food stores carry both regular white chocolate chips, which contain dairy, as well as non-dairy versions. There are also a few brands of non-dairy white chocolate chips online (check Amazon.com). Be sure to read the ingredients and decide which type is best for you.

1. Preheat your oven to 350°F.

2. In a medium-sized bowl, combine the almond flour, coconut flour, arrowroot starch, baking soda, and sea salt.

3. Add the maple syrup, vanilla extract, and egg, and blend with a hand mixer until combined.

4. Add the coconut oil, and blend again to incorporate.

5. Stir in the orange zest, white chocolate chips, and nuts.

6. Scoop rounded tablespoons of dough onto a parchment-lined baking sheet. Flatten each dough ball slightly with the palm of your hand since these cookies don't spread while baking. (Note: If you use butter instead of coconut oil, they will spread, so be sure to leave space between them).

7. Bake the cookies for 13-15 minutes or until the edges are golden brown.

8. Let the cookies cool on wire racks.

9. Store the cookies in an airtight container, or freeze them until needed.

Lemon Blueberry Coolers

These refreshing cookies make a wonderful treat with tea or coffee on a relaxing Sunday morning. I love to make them in the spring and summer when I'm ready for the lighter flavors of lemon and blueberries. Dehydrated blueberries are an excellent addition because they are concentrated for a pop of blueberry flavor in each bite. Plus, they won't water down the dough or turn it blue! It takes only a few minutes in the batter for the blueberries to soften to perfection.

1. Preheat your oven to 350°F.
2. In a medium-sized bowl, combine the almond flour, coconut flour, arrowroot starch, baking soda, and sea salt.
3. Add the maple syrup, vanilla extract, egg, and lemon juice, and blend with a hand mixer.
4. Slowly add the coconut oil, and blend well.
5. Stir in the lemon zest and blueberries.
6. Let the dough rest for 5 minutes.
7. Stir the dough once more, and scoop it into 1-inch balls. Place the balls on a parchment-lined baking sheet.
8. Bake for 10-12 minutes or until the centers are done and the edges are golden brown.
9. Place the baking sheet on a cooling rack, and let the cookies cool completely.
10. For the frosting, combine the coconut butter, maple syrup, and lemon juice in a small bowl and stir until smooth. If the coconut butter is too thick or hard, microwave it in 10-second increments until it is runny enough to mix well. If the frosting is too thin, refrigerate it briefly until it is thick enough to spread.
11. Spread the frosting on the tops of the cookies, and serve.
12. Store the cookies in an airtight container, or freeze them until ready to eat.

Salted Chocolate Cherry Jumbles

- 2 egg whites
- Pinch of sea salt
- 1 tsp pure vanilla extract
- ⅛ tsp pure almond extract
- 2 TBSP coconut flour, sifted
- ¼ cup almond flour
- ¼ cup cocoa powder
- ⅓ cup pure maple syrup
- ½ cup finely shredded coconut, unsweetened
- ⅓ cup dried cherries, chopped
- ¼ cup toasted almonds, chopped
- ¼ cup mini chocolate chips

Makes 12 cookies

Chocolate. Cherries. Sea salt. This may be the best cookie combination ever! These simple drop cookies are easy and fun to make, especially for the kiddos. So ask little hands to help, and you'll whip these up in no time!

1. Preheat your oven to 350°F.

2. In a medium-sized bowl, beat the egg whites and sea salt with a hand mixer until frothy.

3. Add the vanilla extract, almond extract, coconut flour, almond flour, cocoa powder, and maple syrup. Mix briefly to incorporate.

4. Stir in the coconut, cherries, almonds, and chocolate chips.

5. Scoop rounded tablespoons of dough onto a parchment-lined baking sheet.

6. Bake for 12-15 minutes or until the cookies are firm to the touch and the bottoms are browned.

7. Let the cookies cool on wire racks.

8. Store the cookies in an airtight container, or freeze them until ready to eat.

Almond Orange Biscotti

DRY INGREDIENTS

- ¼ cup coconut sugar
- 1½ cups almond flour
- ¼ cup coconut flour, sifted
- ⅓ cup tapioca starch
- ⅓ cup arrowroot starch, plus more for dusting
- ½ cup coarsely chopped raw almonds
- ½ tsp sea salt

WET INGREDIENTS

- ¼ cup pure maple syrup
- ½ tsp pure almond extract
- 2 TBSP orange juice
- Zest of 1 orange
- ¼ cup coconut oil, melted

COATING INGREDIENTS

- ½ cup chopped dark chocolate or chocolate chips
- ½ tsp pure vanilla extract
- ½ tsp orange extract (optional)
- 2 tsp palm shortening

Makes 8 biscotti

I used to adore a particular locally made biscotti that had a hint of orange flavor and was generously dipped in dark chocolate. Alongside my large-o mocha of sugar and chocolate, it's no wonder I battled with my weight back then. Now I make my own grain-free treats. They have a shorter ingredient list but all the flavor of the real deal! These yummy, crunchy biscotti are perfect with a cup of tea or coffee on a quiet afternoon. Or so I hear.

1. Preheat your oven to 350°F.

2. In a coffee grinder or food processor, grind the coconut sugar into a powder.

3. In a medium-sized bowl, combine the powdered coconut sugar with the almond flour, coconut flour, tapioca starch, arrowroot starch, almonds, and sea salt.

4. Add the maple syrup, almond extract, orange juice, and orange zest, and blend well with a hand mixer.

5. Slowly add the coconut oil, and blend again until incorporated.

6. Let the batter rest for 5 minutes.

7. Spoon the dough onto a parchment-lined baking sheet. Dust your hands lightly with arrowroot starch to prevent sticking and use your hands to shape the dough into a 1-inch-thick rectangle.

8. Bake for 25 minutes.

9. Remove the baking sheet from the oven, and carefully cut the dough into 8 bars, separating them from each other with the knife.

10. Reduce the heat to 275°F, and bake the biscotti for an additional 25-30 minutes or until they are dark golden brown and very firm to the touch.

11. Remove the baking sheet from the oven, and cool the biscotti on the sheet for 20 minutes. Then transfer them to a wire rack to cool completely.

12. Meanwhile, make the chocolate coating. In the top of a double boiler, combine the chocolate, vanilla extract, orange extract, and palm shortening over simmering water. Stir until completely melted.

13. Dip the ends of the cooled biscotti in the melted chocolate, or drizzle the chocolate over the tops of the biscotti. Place the cookies on a wax paper-lined baking sheet until the chocolate hardens.

14. Store the biscotti in an airtight container, or freeze them until ready to eat.

No-Bake Sunbutter Bars

BAR INGREDIENTS

- 1 cup sunbutter (roasted, no sugar)
- ½ cup coconut butter
- 3 TBSP honey
- 1 cup finely shredded coconut, unsweetened
- 2 TBSP cocoa powder
- 3 TBSP coconut oil, melted

TOPPING INGREDIENTS

- ½ cup chopped dark chocolate
- 2 TBSP roasted, salted sunflower seeds

Makes 16 bars

The only thing I have to say about these bars is "Holy delicious!" If you miss those Reese's Peanut Butter Cup days, this is the recipe for you. It's so easy to make, yet it's loaded with delicious, nutritious ingredients. These bars are perfect for the cooler, school lunches, or your next special occasion (say, a 10:00 a.m. tea break with the house all to yourself. Oooh, I love those!). If you prefer almond butter, feel free to use that instead of sunbutter. Then top the bars with sliced roasted almonds instead of sunflower seeds.

1. In a medium-sized bowl, blend the sunbutter, coconut butter, honey, shredded coconut, cocoa powder, and coconut oil until well combined.

2. Press the mixture into a greased 8" x 8" pan, and refrigerate it until firm.

3. Meanwhile, melt the dark chocolate in a microwave-safe bowl or in the top of a double boiler over simmering water.

4. Spread the melted chocolate over the bars, and sprinkle the sunflower seeds over the tops. The chocolate hardens fast on the cooled filling, so you will need to move quickly!

5. Cut into 16 bars. Keep refrigerated or in a cooler until ready to eat. You can also freeze the bars in an airtight container for later use.

Chocolate Chip Tahini Blondies with Toasted Coconut

DRY INGREDIENTS

- 1½ cups almond flour
- ⅓ cup arrowroot starch
- ¾ tsp baking soda
- ¼ tsp sea salt

WET INGREDIENTS

- ⅓ cup pure maple syrup
- ¼ cup tahini
- 1 egg (or 2 TBSP warmed applesauce mixed with ½ tsp baking powder)
- 1 TBSP pure vanilla extract
- 2 TBSP coconut oil, melted

ADD-IN

- ½ cup dark chocolate chips

TOPPINGS

- ½ cup finely shredded coconut, unsweetened
- 2 TBSP mini chocolate chips

Makes 16 bars

I keep asking myself why I didn't think to create these chewy, dense bars of yumminess sooner! The added tahini provides a beautiful crumb and chewy texture without altering the flavor of the bars. So. Darn. Good! And if you need a nut-free version, I've made these with homemade raw sunflower seed flour (see page 28 for more information) instead of almond flour, and they were just as delicious. You can make so many variations from this basic recipe too. Add nuts or raisins, or substitute almond butter or sunbutter for the tahini. The options are endless!

1. Preheat your oven to 350°F.
2. Line an 8" x 8" glass baking dish with parchment paper, and grease it.
3. In a medium-sized bowl, combine the dry ingredients.
4. Add the maple syrup, tahini, egg, and vanilla extract, and mix well with a hand mixer.
5. Add the coconut oil, and blend again to incorporate.
6. Stir in the dark chocolate chips.
7. Spread the dough evenly in the prepared baking dish.
8. Sprinkle the coconut and mini chocolate chips on top, and lightly press them into the dough with your palm.
9. Bake the blondies for 23-25 minutes or until the edges are golden brown and the center is firm and springs back when pressed with your finger.
10. Let the blondies cool for 45 minutes on a wire rack.
11. Pull the bars out of the dish by the edges of the parchment paper. Place them on a cooling rack, and let them cool completely before slicing into 16 bars.
12. Store the bars in an airtight container, or freeze them until needed.

Pumpkin Pie Bars

CRUST INGREDIENTS

- 1½ cups raw walnuts or pecans
- ¼ cup coconut flour, sifted
- ¼ cup arrowroot starch
- Pinch of sea salt
- 1 egg
- 2 TBSP pure maple syrup

FILLING INGREDIENTS

- 1½ cups pumpkin puree (15-ounce can)
- 1½ tsp cinnamon
- ¼ tsp nutmeg
- ¼ tsp ground ginger
- ¼ tsp ground cloves
- 1 tsp arrowroot starch
- Pinch of sea salt
- ⅓ cup pure maple syrup
- 3 eggs
- 2 tsp pure vanilla extract
- ¼ cup coconut milk

TOPPING INGREDIENTS

- 1 cup raw walnuts or pecans, coarsely chopped
- ¼ cup almond flour
- ¼ tsp cinnamon
- 1 TBSP pure maple syrup
- 1 TBSP coconut oil, melted

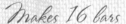

Makes 16 bars

This recipe has quite a few ingredients, but it's oh-so-easy to throw together! And oh-so-worth the few minutes of prep. This fall-infused bar brings the best of a pumpkin pie, cookie, and crumble into one delectable, handheld treat. It's great for holiday parties or anytime you want the taste of autumn.

1. Preheat your oven to 350°F.
2. Make the crust. In a food processor, pulse the walnuts or pecans into a coarse meal.
3. In a small bowl, combine the chopped nuts, coconut flour, arrowroot starch, and sea salt.
4. Add the egg and maple syrup to the bowl, and mix well.
5. Grease an 8" x 8" glass dish with coconut oil or ghee. Press the crust mixture evenly into the dish. You will want to grease your hands well so that the batter doesn't stick to your skin.
6. Bake the bars for 12-14 minutes or until they are golden brown and the center is set.
7. Meanwhile, in a large bowl, mix the filling ingredients until well blended and smooth.
8. In a small bowl, combine the topping ingredients, and mix well with a spoon.
9. When the crust is done, remove it from the oven, and pour the filling over the hot crust.
10. Sprinkle the topping evenly over the filling. Bake for an additional 40-45 minutes or until the center is set.
11. Let cool completely before slicing into bars.
12. Store the bars in an airtight container in the refrigerator. You can also freeze the cooled bars in an airtight container or freezer bag until needed.

Cherry Pistachio Scones

DRY INGREDIENTS
- 1 cup shelled pistachios, coarsely chopped
- ¾ cup almond flour
- 3 TBSP coconut flour, sifted
- ¼ cup arrowroot starch + 1 TBSP for dusting
- ¼ tsp sea salt

WET INGREDIENTS
- 2 eggs
- ⅓ cup pure maple syrup
- 1 tsp pure vanilla extract
- ⅛ tsp pure almond extract
- 2 TBSP coconut oil, melted

ADD-IN
- 1 cup dried cherries

Makes 8 scones

I have a new favorite scone recipe. Wanna know what it is? Yep, it's this one! The texture of these scones is spot-on, and the pistachios give them an extra layer of flavor. Then you bite into a tart cherry! Oh my! I really need a cup of coffee and one of these bad boys right now.

1. Preheat your oven to 350°F.
2. Line a baking sheet with parchment paper.
3. In a medium-sized bowl, combine the pistachios, almond flour, coconut flour, ¼ cup arrowroot starch, and sea salt.
4. Add the eggs, maple syrup, vanilla extract, and almond extract, and blend the ingredients with a hand mixer.
5. Slowly add the coconut oil, and mix well.
6. Stir in the dried cherries.
7. Cover and refrigerate the dough for 1 hour.
8. Spoon the dough onto the baking sheet. Dust your hands with 1 TBSP arrowroot starch, and shape the dough into a 2-inch-thick disc.
9. Bake for 20 minutes.
10. Remove the baking sheet from the oven, and very carefully cut the dough into 8 wedges, gently sliding the wedges apart with the knife. Bake for an additional 8-10 minutes or until the scones are golden brown and firm to the touch.
11. Let the scones cool completely on the baking sheet placed on a wire rack.
12. Store the scones in an airtight container, or freeze them until ready to eat.

Elvis Muffins

Poor Elvis. A few not-so-great years, and how quickly we forget the amazing songs and movies from the first decade of his career! Though the math doesn't add up (I'm only 29 . . . again), as a girl, I watched reruns of some of his happy-go-lucky movies such as Blue Hawaii and Jailhouse Rock. They were fun, innocent entertainment, which I think we need a little more of today. But the one thing I've always been curious about is whether Elvis really did eat peanut butter, banana, and bacon sandwiches! This is vital information, and I think we need answers. In the meantime, here's a Paleo nod to the King of Rock and Roll!

TOPPING INGREDIENTS
- 6 strips bacon
- 1 TBSP pure maple syrup

DRY INGREDIENTS
- ¾ cup almond flour
- ⅓ cup coconut flour, sifted
- 2 TBSP arrowroot starch
- ¾ tsp baking soda
- ½ tsp cinnamon
- Pinch of sea salt

WET INGREDIENTS
- 4 eggs
- 2 tsp pure vanilla extract
- ¼ cup pure maple syrup
- 2 overripe small bananas, mashed (about ½ cup)
- ½ cup coconut milk (if needed)
- ¼ cup coconut oil, melted

ADD-IN
- ½ cup almond butter or sunbutter

Makes 12 muffins

1. Preheat your oven to 400°F.

2. Lay the bacon on a baking sheet. Drizzle maple syrup over each strip, and use your hands to spread it evenly.

3. Bake the bacon for 15 minutes. Flip the strips, and bake them for 5 more minutes or until the bacon is browned and cooked through but not too crispy.

4. Let the bacon strips cool on the baking sheet. Then crumble them into small pieces.

5. Meanwhile, make the muffins. In a medium-sized bowl, combine the almond flour, coconut flour, baking powder, cinnamon, and sea salt.

6. Add the eggs, vanilla extract, maple syrup, and bananas, and blend with a hand mixer until combined.

7. Slowly add the coconut oil to the bowl, and blend well. If the batter is runny, let it sit for 5 minutes to thicken. If it's too thick, add a small amount of coconut milk and blend again. It should look like a traditional muffin batter.

8. Line muffin tins with paper cups. Fill each muffin cup three-quarters full. Spoon 1 TBSP almond butter into the center of each muffin, and push it gently into the center so that it is covered with batter.

9. Sprinkle the tops of the muffins with the bacon pieces.

10. Bake the muffins for 15 minutes or until they spring back when touched.

11. Let the muffins cool completely on wire racks.

12. Store the muffins in an airtight container, or freeze them until needed. Simply let them thaw to room temperature before eating.

Lemon Coconut Loaf

DRY INGREDIENTS

- 1 cup almond flour
- ¼ cup coconut flour, sifted
- 3 TBSP arrowroot starch
- 1 tsp baking powder
- ¼ tsp baking soda
- ¼ tsp sea salt

WET INGREDIENTS

- 3 eggs
- 1 tsp pure vanilla extract
- ¼ cup pure maple syrup
- ½ cup coconut milk
- ¼ cup coconut oil, melted
- 2 TBSP lemon juice

ADD-INS

- 2 tsp lemon zest
- ⅓ cup finely shredded coconut, unsweetened, plus 2 TBSP for topping

Makes 2 mini loaves

I'm not sure when it happens, but at some point in becoming an adult, your palate changes, and you start to enjoy flavors other than sweet, sweet, and sweeter. I wasn't a fan of lemon-flavored treats as a kid, but as an adult, I can't get enough! Especially once spring hits and the sun shines. Lemons just scream sunshine. This bread is moist on the inside and browned and delicious on the outside. The slight lemon and coconutty flavors blend well to give you a little taste of summer in each bite!

1. Preheat your oven to 350°F.
2. In a medium-sized bowl, combine the dry ingredients.
3. Add the eggs, vanilla extract, maple syrup, coconut milk, coconut oil, and lemon juice, and mix well with a hand mixer.
4. Stir in the lemon zest and ⅓ cup shredded coconut.
5. Grease 2 mini loaf pans (3" x 5¾"), and divide the batter evenly between the 2 pans.
6. Sprinkle 1 TBSP shredded coconut over the top of each loaf.
7. Bake for 35-40 minutes or until the loaves are golden brown and the centers spring back when pressed.
8. Remove the pans from the oven, and let the loaves cool in the pans on a wire rack for 15 minutes.
9. Turn the loaves out onto the wire rack to finish cooling completely.
10. Slice and serve, or freeze the loaves in an airtight container until needed.

Chocolate Chip Banana Bread with Cinnamon Sugar Topping

DRY INGREDIENTS

- 1½ cups almond flour
- ⅓ cup coconut flour, sifted
- ⅓ cup arrowroot starch
- 1 tsp baking soda
- 1 tsp cinnamon
- ½ tsp sea salt

WET INGREDIENTS

- 4 very ripe bananas (the more brown spots, the better; if you use frozen bananas instead of fresh, you may not need all of the coconut milk, so add it slowly until it becomes a thick batter)
- 4 eggs
- 2 tsp pure vanilla extract
- ⅓ cup coconut milk

ADD-IN

- 1 cup chocolate chips

TOPPING INGREDIENTS

- 2 TBSP coconut sugar
- ¾ tsp cinnamon
- 1 TBSP almond flour

Makes 1 loaf

Bananas. Chocolate. Cinnamon. Booyah! The addicting flavor combination of this delightfully tasty classic banana bread will have your family and friends begging for more. But the added cinnamon sugar topping really puts this one over the top. Because it's on the top! Get it? Never mind.

1. Preheat your oven to 350°F.

2. In a small bowl, combine the almond flour, coconut flour, arrowroot starch, baking soda, cinnamon, and sea salt.

3. In a large bowl, blend the bananas, eggs, vanilla extract, and coconut milk with a hand mixer until the bananas are fully mashed and the ingredients are well combined.

4. Add the dry ingredients to the large bowl, and blend until the ingredients are fully incorporated.

5. Stir in the chocolate chips.

6. Grease a 9" x 5" loaf pan. Pour the batter into the greased pan.

7. In a small bowl, combine the topping ingredients and mix well with a spoon. Sprinkle the topping evenly over the batter.

8. Bake the loaf for 55-60 minutes or until the center is set and a toothpick inserted into the center comes out clean.

9. Remove the loaf from the oven, and let it cool for 10 minutes in the pan on a wire rack.

10. Turn the loaf out onto the wire rack to finish cooling.

11. Slice the loaf and serve or store in an airtight container.

12. To store the loaf in the freezer, place small squares of wax paper between the slices. Place the slices in a freezer-safe zip-top bag, and freeze until needed.

13. Simply thaw a slice at time (or the whole loaf) in the refrigerator, and enjoy! I like my bread warm, so I heat it for a few seconds in the microwave before devouring.

Monday

Tuesday

Wednesday

Thursday

Friday

Week in a Day

{ cook once for a
stress-free work week! }

Menu:

MONDAY
Sesame Chicken Salad

TUESDAY
Shredded Pork Tacos with Mango Salsa

WEDNESDAY
Steak Cobb Salad with Mango Dressing

THURSDAY
Bacon Chicken Pizza

FRIDAY
**Pulled Pork Over Cauliflower Rice
with Spicy Tomato Sauce**

Week in a Day

grocery list

- ☑ 5 pound whole chicken
- ☑ 4-5 pounds pork roast (shoulder or loin)
- ☑ 2 pounds steak (ribeyes, sirloin, skirt or flank)
- ☑ 1 can (5.75-ounce) black olives
- ☑ 28-ounce can tomato sauce
- ☑ 2 cans (6-ounce) tomato paste
- ☑ 28-ounce can diced tomatoes
- ☑ 2 yellow onions
- ☑ 1 bunch Italian, flat leaf parsley
- ☑ 1 small shallot
- ☑ 2 bulbs of garlic
- ☑ 1-inch piece ginger root
- ☑ 8-ounce package white button mushrooms
- ☑ 1 bell pepper, any color
- ☑ 1 medium bunch basil
- ☑ 1 head cauliflower
- ☑ 1 head butter or romaine lettuce
- ☑ 1 head green leaf lettuce (or choice)

- ☑ 1 small head green cabbage
- ☑ ½ small head red cabbage
- ☑ 2 carrots
- ☑ 4 green onions
- ☑ 2 avocados
- ☑ 2 large tomatoes on the vine
- ☑ 2 medium mangos
- ☑ 1 small red onion
- ☑ 1 jalapeno
- ☑ 1 medium bunch cilantro
- ☑ 1 lime
- ☑ toasted sesame seeds
- ☑ ½ cup toasted slivered almonds
- ☑ 1 dozen eggs
- ☑ 12 strips bacon (about 1 pound)
- ☑ 2 cups chicken or beef broth
- ☑ coconut aminos
- ☑ honey
- ☑ sesame oil
- ☑ tahini
- ☑ Red Star active dry yeast

Should already have:

- ☑ almond flour
- ☑ apple cider vinegar
- ☑ arrowroot starch
- ☑ coconut flour
- ☑ coconut oil
- ☑ olive oil
- ☑ black pepper
- ☑ sea salt
- ☑ spices

Prep Day:

Make the Chicken

1. Preheat your oven to 425°F.

2. Season the chicken with sea salt and pepper inside and out.

3. On a rack in a shallow roasting pan, place the chicken breast side up. Drizzle melted coconut oil over the bird.

4. Roast the chicken, uncovered, until the skin is golden brown and the juices run clear when pierced, about 1½ hours. An instant-read thermometer should read 180°F in the breast and 190°F in the thigh.

5. Remove the chicken from the oven, and let it rest until it is cool enough to handle.

6. Pull all the meat you can from the chicken, and store it in an airtight container in the refrigerator until needed.

7. Be sure to freeze the carcass to make broth later!

Make the Pork

1. Season the pork with sea salt and pepper, and place it in a slow cooker with the broth.

2. Cook the pork on high for 4 hours.

3. Remove the pork from the slow cooker, and let it rest for 15 minutes.

4. With 2 forks, shred the pork, and store it in an airtight container in the refrigerator until needed.

Make the Red Sauce

1. In a large pot over medium heat, heat the olive oil.

2. Add the onion, and cook until it is soft, about 5 minutes.

3. Stir in the garlic and parsley.

4. Add the tomato sauce, tomato paste, tomatoes, oregano, basil, rosemary, sea salt, and pepper, and stir well to combine.

5. Reduce the heat to low, and simmer the sauce, covered, for 30 minutes.

6. Remove the sauce from the heat and let it cool.

7. Store the cooled sauce in an airtight container in the refrigerator until needed.

CHICKEN
- Whole chicken (5 pounds)
- Sea salt to taste
- Freshly ground black pepper to taste
- 2 TBSP coconut oil, melted

PORK
- 5 pounds pork roast
- Sea salt to taste
- Freshly ground black pepper to taste
- 2 cups chicken or beef broth

RED SAUCE
- ¼ cup olive oil
- 1 small onion, diced
- 1 clove garlic, minced
- ¼ cup chopped parsley
- 1 can (28-ounce) tomato sauce
- 2 cans (6-ounce) tomato paste
- 1 can (28-ounce) diced tomatoes
- ½ tsp oregano
- ½ tsp basil
- Pinch of rosemary
- 1 tsp sea salt
- Freshly ground black pepper to taste

SESAME DRESSING

- 1 small shallot, minced
- 1 tsp grated fresh ginger
- ⅔ cup olive oil
- ¼ cup apple cider vinegar
- 2 TBSP coconut aminos
- 1 TBSP honey
- 2 tsp sesame oil
- 1 TBSP tahini
- Freshly ground black pepper to taste

MANGO SALSA

- 2 medium ripe mangoes, peeled, seeds removed, and diced
- ¼ cup diced red onion
- 1 jalapeño, cored, seeded, and diced
- 1 clove garlic, minced
- 2 TBSP chopped fresh cilantro
- 2 TBSP chopped fresh parsley
- 2 tsp lime juice
- ¼ tsp sea salt
- Pinch of freshly ground black pepper

STEAK

- 2 ribeye steaks, about 2 pounds
- Sea salt to taste
- Freshly ground black pepper to taste

BOILED EGGS

- 4 eggs

BACON

- 12 strips bacon

Make the Sesame Dressing

1. In a jar with a tight-fitting lid, combine all the ingredients.
2. Shake vigorously to mix, and store the dressing in the refrigerator until needed.

Make the Mango Salsa

1. In a medium-sized bowl, combine all the ingredients. Stir gently.
2. Store the salsa in an airtight container in the refrigerator until needed.

Make the Steak

1. Heat the grill.
2. Season the steaks with sea salt and pepper.
3. Grill the steaks for about 4 minutes per side or until they reach medium doneness.
4. Let the steaks rest for 10 minutes.
5. Slice the steaks into strips.
6. Store the steaks in an airtight container in the refrigerator until needed.

Make 2 Pizza Crusts

1. See page 66 for the recipe. Place the cooled crusts in a 1-gallon freezer bag, and freeze until needed.

Boil the Eggs for the Salad

1. In a small saucepan, cover the eggs with cold water, and turn the heat to medium.
2. Bring the water to a boil, and boil the eggs for 2 minutes.
3. Remove the eggs from the heat, cover, and let them sit for 12 minutes.
4. Rinse the eggs in the pan in cold water until they are cool enough to peel.
5. Gently peel the eggs, and store them in an airtight container in the refrigerator until needed.

Bake the Bacon for the Salad and Pizza

1. Preheat your oven to 375°F.

2. On a large baking sheet, spread the bacon evenly.

3. Bake the bacon for 15 minutes.

4. Remove the bacon from the oven, and flip the slices over. Bake for another 10 minutes. Keep an eye on it, as bacon can go from not even close to burned very quickly!

5. If necessary, flip the bacon again, and bake for another 3-4 minutes.

6. When done, let the bacon cool.

7. Chop the bacon, and store it in an airtight container in the refrigerator until needed.

Monday
Sesame Chicken Salad

- *Half of the cooked chicken meat
- 1 small head green cabbage, core removed, sliced thin
- 1 cup thinly sliced red cabbage
- 2 medium carrots, julienned
- 4 green onions, sliced
- 3 TBSP toasted sesame seeds
- ½ cup toasted slivered almonds
- *Sesame Dressing

*Ingredients made on Prep Day

Serves 4

1. In a large bowl, combine the chicken, cabbage, carrots, onions, sesame seeds, and almonds.

2. Remove the Sesame Dressing from the refrigerator, shake the jar vigorously to combine, and pour the dressing over the salad.

3. Toss to coat the salad ingredients with the dressing, and serve.

- 3 TBSP coconut oil
- *Half of the shredded pork
- 1 TBSP Taco Seasoning (page 39)
- ¼ cup water
- Butter lettuce or romaine lettuce leaves
- *Half of the Mango Salsa

Ingredients made on "Prep Day"

Serves 4

Tuesday
Shredded Pork Tacos with Mango Salsa

1. In a large skillet over medium heat, heat the coconut oil.

2. Add the shredded pork, and stir to coat the pork with the oil.

3. Add the Taco Seasoning and water, and stir to combine.

4. Reduce the heat to low, and simmer, uncovered, until the pork is heated through.

5. Serve the shredded pork in lettuce cups with Mango Salsa spooned on top.

Wednesday
Steak Cobb Salad with Mango Dressing

SALAD

- 6 cups lettuce torn into bite-sized pieces
- *Steak strips
- *4 boiled eggs, sliced
- 2 avocados, diced
- 2 cups chopped tomatoes or cherry tomatoes
- *Half of the crumbled bacon

DRESSING

- *Half of the Mango Salsa
- ⅓ cup olive oil
- 2 TBSP apple cider vinegar
- ¼ cup water

Ingredients made on "Prep Day"

Serves 4

1. Divide the lettuce among 4 serving bowls.

2. Layer each bowl with the steak, eggs, avocados, tomatoes, and bacon.

3. In a food processor, purée the Mango Salsa, olive oil, apple cider vinegar, and water until smooth. If you prefer a thinner dressing, add more water, and process again.

4. Spoon the dressing over each salad, and enjoy!

Thursday
Bacon Chicken Pizza

- *2 pizza crusts, thawed
- *Half of the Red Sauce
- *Half of the cooked chicken meat
- 1 cup sliced mushrooms
- 1 cup sliced black olives
- 1 cup chopped bell pepper, any color
- *Half of the crumbled bacon
- ½ cup fresh basil leaves torn into bite-sized pieces

Ingredients made on "Prep Day"

Serves 4

1. Preheat your oven to 375°F.

2. Place crusts on a baking sheet. Spread the Red Sauce on each pizza crust. Top with the chicken, mushrooms, olives, peppers, and bacon, or any of your other favorite toppings.

3. Bake for 10-15 minutes or until the toppings are hot and the sauce bubbles. The more toppings you use, the longer the pizzas will take to bake.

4. Sprinkle fresh basil over each pizza, cut into slices, and serve!

Pulled Pork
over Cauliflower Rice
with Spicy Tomato Sauce

PULLED PORK & SAUCE

- *Half of the shredded pork
- *Half of the Red Sauce
- 1 tsp red pepper flakes

CAULIFLOWER RICE

- 2 TBSP coconut oil
- ¼ cup diced yellow onion
- 1 head cauliflower, washed, stem removed, coarsely chopped

Ingredients made on "Prep Day"

Serves 4

1. In a large pot over low heat, combine the pork, Red Sauce, and crushed red pepper. Cook, stirring occasionally, until the ingredients are heated through.

2. Meanwhile, make the Cauliflower Rice. Place the chopped cauliflower in a food processor, and pulse until it is finely chopped to the size of grains of rice.

3. In a large skillet over medium heat, melt the coconut oil.

4. Add the diced onion, and cook, stirring occasionally, until softened, about 4 minutes.

5. Add the cauliflower to the skillet, and stir.

6. Reduce the heat to low, cover, and cook for 5-10 minutes or until softened but not mushy.

7. To serve, place a spoonful of Cauliflower Rice on 4 plates, and spoon the pork/sauce mixture over each.

85% Dark Chocolate	www.greenandblacks.com
Almond Flour	www.honeyvillegrain.com
Apple Cider Vinegar	www.bragg.com
Arrowroot Starch	www.bobsredmill.com
Artisan Bistro Frozen Meals	www.artisanbistropro.com/pc530473
Broth (recipe)	www.nomnompaleo.com
Chestnut Flour	www.oregonchestnuts.com
Chomps Snack Sticks	www.gochomps.com
Chocolate Chips	www.enjoylifefoods.com
Coconut Milk (canned)	www.naturalvalue.com and Trader Joe's
Coconut Oil	www.wildernessfamilynaturals.com and tropicaltraditions.com
Coconut: Shredded, Flakes, Butter	www.edwardandsons.com
Coconut: Sugar, Nectar, Aminos, vinegar, flour	www.coconutsecret.com
Cooking Spray	www.kelapo.com
Duck Fat, Tallow	www.fatworks.wazala.com
Epic Bars	www.epicbar.com
Fermented Foods	www.pickledplanet.com
Fish Sauce	www.thaikitchen.com
Ghee	www.pureindianfoods.com
Honey	www.reallyrawhoney.com
Hot Dogs	www.applegate.com and www.forkintheroad.com
Hot Sauce – Organic Harvest	www.azgunslinger.com
Maple Sugar	www.traderjoes.com and www.coombsfamilyfarms.com
Maple Syrup	www.wholefoods.com and www.coombsfamilyfarms.com
Mashed Potato Flakes	www.edwardandsons.com
Meats	www.grasslandbeef.com and txbarorganics.com
Paleo Ketchup	www.stevespaleogoods.com and in *Everyday Paleo cookbook*
Paleo Kits	www.stevespaleogoods.com
Paleo Mayo (recipe)	www.nomnompaleo.com and *Everyday Paleo cookbook*
Paleo People Granola	www.paleopeople.com
Palm Shortening	www.spectrumorganics.com and www.tropicaltraditions.com
Primal Pacs	www.primalpacs.com
Sea Salt	www.celticseasalt.com and www.realsalt.com
Spices	www.spicely.com
Tahini	www.artisanafoods.com and www.arrowheadmills.com
Tapioca Starch	www.bobsredmill.com and www.bigrivergrains.com
Yeast	www.redstaryeast.com

Cast Iron Cookware	www.lodgemfg.com
Collapsible Containers	www.amazon.com
Cutting Boards	www.kutskokitchen.com
Electric Skillets	www.amazon.com
English Muffin Rings	www.amazon.com
Food Processor	www.cuisinart.com
Glasslock Containers	www.glasslockusa.com
Hand Mixer	www.cuisinart.com
High Speed Blender	www.vitamix.com and www.blendtec.com
Kitchen Scoops	www.amazon.com
Loaf Pans (3" x 5½" & 5½" x 9½")	www.amazon.com
Magic Bullet Blender	www.buythebullet.com
Mason Jars	www.amazon.com
Slow Cookers	www.amazon.com
Splatter Screen	www.amazon.com

 Information Resources

Eat Well Guide	www.eatwellguide.org	Info on where to find local, sustainable, organic food near you.
Eat Wild	www.eatwild.com	Info and links for pastured, grass-fed meats.
Local Harvest	www.localharvest.org	Info on where to find local farmers' markets, family farms, and CSAs near you.
Paleo Magazine	www.paleomagonline.com	First and only print magazine dedicated to the Paleo lifestyle and ancestral health.
Pure Primal Challenge	www.pureprimalchallenge.com	Info and resources to get you started on your paleo journey.
The Healthy GF Life	www.thehealthygflife.com	Find recipes, info, and real life experiences to help you on your GF journey!
WellCOR	www.wellcor.net	Information and assistance with overall wellness.
Weston A. Price Foundation	www.westonaprice.org	Info about the health benefits of organic, biodynamic farming and pasture raised livestock.

Conversion Chart

Unit:	Equals:	Also equals:	Fluid ounces:	Metric equivalent:
1 teaspoon	1/3 tablespoon	1/48 cup	1/6 fl. oz	5 ml
1/16 cup	1 tablespoon	3 teaspoons	1/2 fl. oz	15 ml
1/8 cup	2 tablespoons	6 teaspoons	1 fl. oz	30 ml
1/6 cup	2 tablespoons + 2 teaspoons	8 teaspoons	1 1/3 fl. oz	40 ml
1/4 cup	4 tablespoons	12 teaspoons	2 fl. oz	60 ml
1/3 cup	5 tablespoons + 1 teaspoon	16 teaspoons	2 2/3 fl. oz	80 ml
3/8 cup	6 tablespoons	18 teaspoons	3 fl. oz	90 ml
1/2 cup	8 tablespoons	24 teaspoons	4 fl. oz	120 ml
2/3 cup	10 tablespoons + 2 teaspoons	32 teaspoons	5 1/3 fl. oz	160 ml
3/4 cup	12 tablespoons	36 teaspoons	6 fl. oz	180 ml
1 cup	16 tablespoons	48 teaspoons	8 fl. oz	240 ml
2 cups	1 pint	32 tablespoons	16 fl. oz	470 ml
2 pints	1 quart	4 cups	32 fl. oz	.95 liter
4 quarts	1 gallon (gal)	16 cups	128 fl. oz	3.8 liters

1 milliliter (ml) = 1 cubic centimeter (cc)

1 inch (in) = 2.54 centimeters (cm)

16 ounces (oz) = 1 pound (lb)

1 oz. = 28 grams

1 pound = 454 grams

Fluid Measurement Abbreviations

ml means milliliters
cc is the same as ml
oz means ounce (fluid)
gal means gallon

Weight Measurement Abbreviations

g means grams
lbs means pounds
oz means ounce (weight)

US weight:	Metric equivalent:
1/4 oz	7 g
1/2 oz	15 g
3/4 oz	20 g
1 oz	30 g
8 oz	225 g
12 oz	340 g
16 oz (1 lb)	455 g

Fahrenheit:	Celsius:
32º	0º
180º	82º
212º	100º
250º	120º
350º	175º
425º	220º
500º	260º

index...

about the author...

Tammy Credicott is a recipe developer, food photographer, and the national best-selling author of *Paleo Indulgences* and *The Healthy Gluten-Free Life*. She and her husband owned a successful gluten-free bakery before they were inspired to transform their health further by switching to a Paleo lifestyle. Tammy has a passion for understanding health and wellness as it relates to nutrition and has used this knowledge to help her family overcome health issues such as celiac disease, food allergies, and ADD.

A self-taught home cook extraordinaire and Food Network junkie, Tammy has transformed her family's well-being with the creation of simple, healthy, allergy-friendly—and delicious!—recipes that fit their busy lifestyle. And while some of her favorite things include summer vacation, months ending in "-ber," and photography, she finds her passion and enthusiasm for life in the kitchen with her family. Tammy lives in Bend, Oregon with her husband and two daughters.

 www.facebook.com/thehealthygflife

 www.twitter.com/healthygflife

 www.thehealthygflife.com

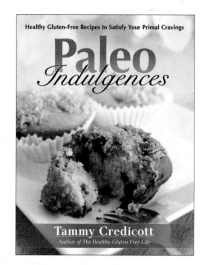 www.pinterest.com/healthygflife

{ Other books by Tammy Credicott: }

The Healthy Gluten-Free Life

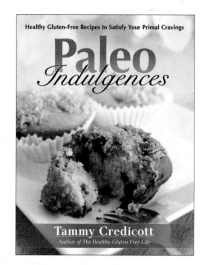

Paleo Indulgences

How to Store Anything

What to Store	Pantry/Countertop	In Fridge	In Freezer	Freezer How-To
FRUITS				
Grapes	no	1 to 2 weeks	8 to 12 months	Wash & pat dry. Spread on tray & freeze until firm. Store in a sealed freezer bag.
Bananas	5 days	2 weeks	8 to 12 months	Peel first. Store 4 bananas per freezer bag for easier measuring.
Berries	no	2 to 7 days	8 to 12 months	Wash and pat dry. Spread on tray & freeze until firm. Store in a sealed freezer bag.
Apples	3 to 4 days	up to 4 months depending on variety	8 to 12 months	Core, peel, slice, & toss in lemon juice to prevent browning. Spread on tray & freeze until firm. Store in a sealed freezer bag.
Cherries	no	3 days	8 to 12 months	Wash, dry and pit. Spread on tray & freeze until firm. Store in a sealed freezer bag.
Melons	3 to 4 days	5 days whole; 3 days cut	6 to 12 months	Cube or slice without rind. Spread on a tray & freeze until firm. Store in a sealed freezer bag.
Peaches/Plums/Nectarines	1 to 2 days	5 days	6 to 12 months	Peel, remove pit & slice. Place on a tray & freeze until firm. Store in a sealed freezer bag.
VEGGIES				
Peppers	no	1 week (green); 5 days (red, yellow, orange)	6 to 9 months	Wash, chop or slice & store in a sealed freezer bag.
Onions	2 months	4 days (cut)	3 to 6 months	Peel, chop & store in a sealed freezer bag.
Sweet Potatoes	2 weeks	3 days (peeled, diced)	2 to 3 months	Peel, dice & store in a sealed freezer bag. Store cooked, cooled and mashed sweet potatoes in airtight containers.
Tomatoes	3 to 4 days	no	no	no
Most Other Veggies	no	1 to 7 days	3 to 6 months	Most veggies like broccoli & cauliflower freeze well after blanching, cooling & drying. Spread on a tray & freeze until firm. Store in a sealed freezer bag.
MEATS/SEAFOOD				
Steak	no	3 days	6 months	Store in freezer bags.
Chops	no	3 days	6 months	Store in freezer bags.
Roasts	no	3 days	6 months	Store in freezer bags.
Ground	no	2 days	4 months	Store in freezer bags.
Bacon	no	2 weeks (unopened); 1 week (opened)	1 month	Store in original packaging placed inside a freezer bag.
Sausage, raw	no	2 days	2 months	Store in freezer bags.
Fish	no	2 days	6 months	Store in freezer bags.
Shellfish	no	2 days	3 to 4 months	Store in freezer bags.
Poultry	no	2 days	4 to 6 months	Store in freezer bags.

How to Store Anything

What to Store	Pantry/Countertop	In Fridge	In Freezer	Freezer How-To
Quick Breads (muffins/pancakes)	no	3 to 4 days	2 to 3 months	Store in freezer bags or airtight container.
Yeast Breads	no	1 to 2 days	3 to 6 months	Store in freezer bags or airtight container.
Coconut Flour	no	6 months	12 months	Store in freezer bags or airtight container.
Almond Flour	no	6 months	12 to 18 months	Store in freezer bags or airtight container.
Starches	1 to 2 months	6 to 8 months	12 to 18 months	Store in freezer bags or airtight container.
Cookies	2 to 3 days	1 week	3 months	Store in freezer bags or airtight container.
Coconut Milk, canned	2 to 3 years (unopened), use by exp. date on can	7 - 10 days in a separate container	3 to 6 months in an a separate container	Store in an airtight container. Leave room at the top for expansion when it freezes.
Ghee	6 months (unopened)	9 to 12 months	12 to 18 months	Store in original container.
Butter, sticks	no	3 months	6 months	Store in original packaging placed inside a freezer bag.
Broth, homemade	no	7 days	3 months	Store in an airtight container. Leave room at the top for expansion when it freezes.
Nuts/Seeds	1 month	6 to 12 months	1 to 2 years	Shell first. Store in an airtight container or freezer bag.
Coconut, shredded	6 months (unopened)	8 to 12 months	12 to 18 months	Store in freezer bags.
Dried Fruits	6 months (unopened)	no	no	no

BAKING

MISC

stocking your paleo kitchen...

When buying pantry items, look for organic products in BPA-free cans or glass containers. This list isn't all-inclusive by any means, but it's a great place to start in turning your SAD kitchen into a Paleo powerhouse! You can find where to buy many of these items in the resource section on page 265.

Pantry:

- ☑ almond flour (not meal)
- ☑ arrowroot starch
- ☑ baking powder
- ☑ baking soda
- ☑ cocoa powder
- ☑ coconut butter
- ☑ coconut flour
- ☑ coconut milk (full fat with no carrageenan)
- ☑ coconut oil, virgin (tastes like coconut) and refined (doesn't taste like coconut)
- ☑ nuts and seeds
- ☑ olive oil
- ☑ parchment paper
- ☑ pure almond extract
- ☑ pure maple syrup
- ☑ pure vanilla extract
- ☑ raw honey
- ☑ tapioca starch
- ☑ tomatoes (diced, paste, sauce)
- ☑ tuna, salmon, crab, etc.
- ☑ vinegars (balsamic, coconut, raw apple cider, red wine, white wine)

Spice rack:

- ☑ allspice
- ☑ basil
- ☑ bay leaves
- ☑ black peppercorns (buy a grinder)
- ☑ cardamom
- ☑ chili powder
- ☑ chipotle chili powder
- ☑ cinnamon
- ☑ coriander
- ☑ cumin
- ☑ dill
- ☑ granulated garlic
- ☑ granulated onion
- ☑ ground mustard
- ☑ Italian seasoning
- ☑ marjoram
- ☑ nutmeg
- ☑ oregano
- ☑ paprika
- ☑ rosemary (ground)
- ☑ sea salt (Celtic, pink Himalayan, Real Salt)
- ☑ smoked paprika
- ☑ thyme
- ☑ turmeric

Refrigerator:

- ☑ coconut aminos
- ☑ duck fat
- ☑ farm-fresh eggs
- ☑ fermented foods (kraut, kimchee, etc.)
- ☑ fish sauce
- ☑ fish and seafood
- ☑ fruits
- ☑ ghee
- ☑ lard
- ☑ meats
- ☑ tallow
- ☑ vegetables

> "One cannot think well, love well, sleep well, if one has not dined well."
> -Virginia Woolf, "A Room of One's Own"

stocking your paleo kitchen...

When buying pantry items, look for organic products in BPA-free cans or glass containers. This list isn't all-inclusive by any means, but it's a great place to start in turning your SAD kitchen into a Paleo powerhouse! You can find where to buy many of these items in the resource section on page 265.

Pantry:

- ☑ almond flour (not meal)
- ☑ arrowroot starch
- ☑ baking powder
- ☑ baking soda
- ☑ cocoa powder
- ☑ coconut butter
- ☑ coconut flour
- ☑ coconut milk (full fat with no carrageenan)
- ☑ coconut oil, virgin (tastes like coconut) and refined (doesn't taste like coconut)
- ☑ nuts and seeds
- ☑ olive oil
- ☑ parchment paper
- ☑ pure almond extract
- ☑ pure maple syrup
- ☑ pure vanilla extract
- ☑ raw honey
- ☑ tapioca starch
- ☑ tomatoes (diced, paste, sauce)
- ☑ tuna, salmon, crab, etc.
- ☑ vinegars (balsamic, coconut, raw apple cider, red wine, white wine)

Spice rack:

- ☑ allspice
- ☑ basil
- ☑ bay leaves
- ☑ black peppercorns (buy a grinder)
- ☑ cardamom
- ☑ chili powder
- ☑ chipotle chili powder
- ☑ cinnamon
- ☑ coriander
- ☑ cumin
- ☑ dill
- ☑ granulated garlic
- ☑ granulated onion
- ☑ ground mustard
- ☑ Italian seasoning
- ☑ marjoram
- ☑ nutmeg
- ☑ oregano
- ☑ paprika
- ☑ rosemary (ground)
- ☑ sea salt (Celtic, pink Himalayan, Real Salt)
- ☑ smoked paprika
- ☑ thyme
- ☑ turmeric

Refrigerator:

- ☑ coconut aminos
- ☑ duck fat
- ☑ farm-fresh eggs
- ☑ fermented foods (kraut, kimchee, etc.)
- ☑ fish sauce
- ☑ fish and seafood
- ☑ fruits
- ☑ ghee
- ☑ lard
- ☑ meats
- ☑ tallow
- ☑ vegetables

> "One cannot think well, love well, sleep well, if one has not dined well."
>
> -Virginia Woolf, "A Room of One's Own"

Make Ahead
PALEO.

grocery list

- ☑ 5 pound whole chicken
- ☑ 4-5 pounds pork roast (shoulder or loin)
- ☑ 2 pounds steak (ribeyes, sirloin, skirt or flank)
- ☑ 1 can (5.75-ounce) black olives
- ☑ 28-ounce can tomato sauce
- ☑ 2 cans (6-ounce) tomato paste
- ☑ 28-ounce can diced tomatoes
- ☑ 2 yellow onions
- ☑ 1 bunch Italian, flat leaf parsley
- ☑ 1 small shallot
- ☑ 2 bulbs of garlic
- ☑ 1-inch piece ginger root
- ☑ 8-ounce package white button mushrooms
- ☑ 1 bell pepper, any color
- ☑ 1 medium bunch basil
- ☑ 1 head cauliflower
- ☑ 1 head butter or romaine lettuce
- ☑ 1 head green leaf lettuce (or choice)

- ☑ 1 small head green cabbage
- ☑ ½ small head red cabbage
- ☑ 2 carrots
- ☑ 4 green onions
- ☑ 2 avocados
- ☑ 2 large tomatoes on the vine
- ☑ 2 medium mangos
- ☑ 1 small red onion
- ☑ 1 jalapeno
- ☑ 1 medium bunch cilantro
- ☑ 1 lime
- ☑ toasted sesame seeds
- ☑ ½ cup toasted slivered almonds
- ☑ 1 dozen eggs
- ☑ 12 strips bacon (about 1 pound)
- ☑ 2 cups chicken or beef broth
- ☑ coconut aminos
- ☑ honey
- ☑ sesame oil
- ☑ tahini
- ☑ Red Star active dry yeast

Should already have:

- ☑ almond flour
- ☑ apple cider vinegar
- ☑ arrowroot starch
- ☑ coconut flour
- ☑ coconut oil
- ☑ olive oil
- ☑ black pepper
- ☑ sea salt
- ☑ spices

grocery list

- ☑ 5 pound whole chicken
- ☑ 4-5 pounds pork roast (shoulder or loin)
- ☑ 2 pounds steak (ribeyes, sirloin, skirt or flank)
- ☑ 1 can (5.75-ounce) black olives
- ☑ 28-ounce can tomato sauce
- ☑ 2 cans (6-ounce) tomato paste
- ☑ 28-ounce can diced tomatoes
- ☑ 2 yellow onions
- ☑ 1 bunch Italian, flat leaf parsley
- ☑ 1 small shallot
- ☑ 2 bulbs of garlic
- ☑ 1-inch piece ginger root
- ☑ 8-ounce package white button mushrooms
- ☑ 1 bell pepper, any color
- ☑ 1 medium bunch basil
- ☑ 1 head cauliflower
- ☑ 1 head butter or romaine lettuce
- ☑ 1 head green leaf lettuce (or choice)

- ☑ 1 small head green cabbage
- ☑ ½ small head red cabbage
- ☑ 2 carrots
- ☑ 4 green onions
- ☑ 2 avocados
- ☑ 2 large tomatoes on the vine
- ☑ 2 medium mangos
- ☑ 1 small red onion
- ☑ 1 jalapeno
- ☑ 1 medium bunch cilantro
- ☑ 1 lime
- ☑ toasted sesame seeds
- ☑ ½ cup toasted slivered almonds
- ☑ 1 dozen eggs
- ☑ 12 strips bacon (about 1 pound)
- ☑ 2 cups chicken or beef broth
- ☑ coconut aminos
- ☑ honey
- ☑ sesame oil
- ☑ tahini
- ☑ Red Star active dry yeast

Should already have:

- ☑ almond flour
- ☑ apple cider vinegar
- ☑ arrowroot starch
- ☑ coconut flour
- ☑ coconut oil
- ☑ olive oil
- ☑ black pepper
- ☑ sea salt
- ☑ spices

grocery list

- ☑ 5 pound whole chicken
- ☑ 4-5 pounds pork roast (shoulder or loin)
- ☑ 2 pounds steak (ribeyes, sirloin, skirt or flank)
- ☑ 1 can (5.75-ounce) black olives
- ☑ 28-ounce can tomato sauce
- ☑ 2 cans (6-ounce) tomato paste
- ☑ 28-ounce can diced tomatoes
- ☑ 2 yellow onions
- ☑ 1 bunch Italian, flat leaf parsley
- ☑ 1 small shallot
- ☑ 2 bulbs of garlic
- ☑ 1-inch piece ginger root
- ☑ 8-ounce package white button mushrooms
- ☑ 1 bell pepper, any color
- ☑ 1 medium bunch basil
- ☑ 1 head cauliflower
- ☑ 1 head butter or romaine lettuce
- ☑ 1 head green leaf lettuce (or choice)

- ☑ 1 small head green cabbage
- ☑ ½ small head red cabbage
- ☑ 2 carrots
- ☑ 4 green onions
- ☑ 2 avocados
- ☑ 2 large tomatoes on the vine
- ☑ 2 medium mangos
- ☑ 1 small red onion
- ☑ 1 jalapeno
- ☑ 1 medium bunch cilantro
- ☑ 1 lime
- ☑ toasted sesame seeds
- ☑ ½ cup toasted slivered almonds
- ☑ 1 dozen eggs
- ☑ 12 strips bacon (about 1 pound)
- ☑ 2 cups chicken or beef broth
- ☑ coconut aminos
- ☑ honey
- ☑ sesame oil
- ☑ tahini
- ☑ Red Star active dry yeast

Should already have:

- ☑ almond flour
- ☑ apple cider vinegar
- ☑ arrowroot starch
- ☑ coconut flour
- ☑ coconut oil
- ☑ olive oil
- ☑ black pepper
- ☑ sea salt
- ☑ spices

grocery list

☑ 5 pound whole chicken

☑ 4-5 pounds pork roast (shoulder or loin)

☑ 2 pounds steak (ribeyes, sirloin, skirt or flank)

☑ 1 can (5.75-ounce) black olives

☑ 28-ounce can tomato sauce

☑ 2 cans (6-ounce) tomato paste

☑ 28-ounce can diced tomatoes

☑ 2 yellow onions

☑ 1 bunch Italian, flat leaf parsley

☑ 1 small shallot

☑ 2 bulbs of garlic

☑ 1-inch piece ginger root

☑ 8-ounce package white button mushrooms

☑ 1 bell pepper, any color

☑ 1 medium bunch basil

☑ 1 head cauliflower

☑ 1 head butter or romaine lettuce

☑ 1 head green leaf lettuce (or choice)

☑ 1 small head green cabbage

☑ ½ small head red cabbage

☑ 2 carrots

☑ 4 green onions

☑ 2 avocados

☑ 2 large tomatoes on the vine

☑ 2 medium mangos

☑ 1 small red onion

☑ 1 jalapeno

☑ 1 medium bunch cilantro

☑ 1 lime

☑ toasted sesame seeds

☑ ½ cup toasted slivered almonds

☑ 1 dozen eggs

☑ 12 strips bacon (about 1 pound)

☑ 2 cups chicken or beef broth

☑ coconut aminos

☑ honey

☑ sesame oil

☑ tahini

☑ Red Star active dry yeast

Should already have:

☑ almond flour

☑ apple cider vinegar

☑ arrowroot starch

☑ coconut flour

☑ coconut oil

☑ olive oil

☑ black pepper

☑ sea salt

☑ spices